UNPACKING PAULA
VOLUME I

UNPACKING PAULA
VOLUME I

by

Paula Walborsky

Published by Pointillist Press, Tallahassee, FL, USA

Copyright 2023, Paula Walborsky

All rights reserved. No part of this book may be reproduced or transmitted in any form or by any means, electronic or mechanical, including photocopying, recording or by any information storage and retrieval system, without written permission from the publisher, except for the inclusion of brief quotations in a review.

This is not a book of fiction, but it also is not a history. These are my memories, to the best of my ability. They are my opinions. No one else is responsible for these opinions, these memories, but myself. They are as true as I know how to make them.

When you turn the corner
And you run into yourself
Then you know that you have turned
All the corners that are left.

-Langston Hughes

To Kent, the sun in my solar system.

To my grandchildren, Emily, Charlotte, Gavin, and Beckett. You cannot be loved by too many people.

To all my wonderful friends and relatives who encouraged me, laughed and cried with me. Those who read my posts and suggested I collect them into a book. To Rachel Carrera, Leslie Noyes, Josephine and Royal Yu, Southernmost, my one-of-a-kind brother Marty, and the world's best sister-in-law, Beth.

Other Books by Paula Walborsky:

Unpacking Paula, Volume II

Unpacking Paula, Volume III

Dear Reader,

I have been writing most of my life. Like most people, my mind sometimes returns to the same subject. Some memories, some thoughts seem to come to the paper almost of their own volition. Others, oh, look! There's a squirrel. Compiling them has really been difficult because I, of course, want you to have the joy of every single word of my deathless prose. I finally settled on a more or less alphabetized collection. They were written in random order, and alphabetized by title is about as random as it gets. My wonderful editor, Rachel Carrera, who will be awarded the purple heart with oak clusters for guiding me through this, is not at fault for any non sequiturs. There are three volumes, but the essays are NOT in chronological order. Again, random. That is how they were written. That is how they should be read.

Warmly,

Paula Walborsky

Contents

Dramatis Personae: Who Are These People?	1
2020	3
Abortion	7
The Agenda	9
Aging	11
Ahhhhhhh	13
Alternative Lives	15
Amaryllis	17
Amazon	19
And Another One Bites the Dust	21
Covid Chronicles 1: 3/27/20	25
And So I Came to Tallahassee	27
And So It Goes	33
Another Fall	37
Another Monday	41
Another Trip Around the Sun	43
Aphasia	45
The Art of Lying	47
August 2022	51
August 5, 1943	53
Covid Chronicles 2: 3/28/20	55
Ballerina	57
Bangs	59
The Bathing Suit Brouhaha	61
A Beginner's Clay Animal	63
Birds	65
Birthdays	67

The Blessedly Common Cold	69
A Blood Sport	71
A Bloomin' Genius	73
Body Language	75
Covid Chronicles 3: 3/31/20	77
Bonus Child's Birthday	79
Book Report	81
Born to Rumble	83
Boutique Geri	87
Bridge	91
But I'm Not Finished	93
Butterscotch	95
The Calm After the Storm	97
Cell Phones	101
Cell Phones, the Sequel	103
Covid Chronicles 4: A Pandemic Letter to Mom and Dad	105
Chat	109
Choosing to Be Happy	111
Christmas	113
Cinnamon	115
Clara	119
The Cliff	121
Clutter	123
Color	125
Cooking with Molly	127
Covid Chronicles 5: 4/13/20	129
Creation	133
Dad's 98th Memorial	135
Dancing With Harry	137

The Day After	139
Dear President Biden	141
Dearest Ring	145
The Death of Hope	147
The Denim Bridge	151
Distracted	153
Dr. Fauci Day	155
Covid Chronicles 6: 4/27/20	157
Dragons Love Tacos	161
Edgar Booth	163
Eighteenth Anniversary of Harry's Death	167
Election Day	171
Enforced Sensibility	173
ER	175
Eric	179
Every Day is Prologue	181
The Exclamation Point!	183
An Existential Question	185
Covid Chronicles 7: 5/21/20	187
Falling	191
Family	193
Family Zoom	195
Feast of Words	197
Feet	199
Fifteen, and Counting	201
Figaro	205
First Show	207
The First Time	209
Flash Fiction	213

Covid Chronicles 8: A Covid Calendar: 6/28/20	215
Flash Mob	219
Flowers For Algernon	221
Forgiveness	223
Franklin and Eleanor	225
Fremont, Ohio	229
Friday	231
From Hutchinson to Yokohama	233
FSU, Florida State University	237
The Gardening Gene	239
Gerry	243
Covid Chronicles 9: 6/28/20	247
Leap Year, 2020	249
Mother's Day I	253
Obituary for Myself	255
Orchids on Rosa	257
Winter: Visiting Dad	259
Southernmost	271
Thanksgiving 2020	273
Thanksgiving In a Pandemic	279
Too Much Information	283
Top of the Heap	285
Tri-Hi-Y	289
Covid Chronicles 10: 7/12/20	291
About the Author	293

Dramatis Personae: Who Are These People?

What we have here is the result of lots of electro-chemical brain discharges. They are random. Sometimes I was envisioning a reader. Most often I was not. So, here is a list of the players on my personal stage. Some have long ago exited stage right, leaving holes of various sizes in my heart. Others have endured for decades.

1. **Kent Putnam.** He is my husband and the sun in my solar system.

2. **Harry Walborsky.** My late husband was born the same year as my dad. We were happily married for thirty-two years. He died in 2002. Harry has four children and two grandchildren.

3. **Gerry Levitt** is my mother. She died in 2003, eleven months after Harry.

4. **Ben Levitt** is my father. He died in 2008.

5. **Larry Levitt** is my brother. He died in 2000. He was two years younger. He was married to **Kay**, and they had two sons, **Aaron** and **Matt**. Aaron has a son, and Matt has three daughters.

6. **Marty Levitt** is my baby brother. Born in 1953, he will be seventy this year. Marty has two daughters, **Allison**

and **Rachael**. Both are married, and he is a grandfather four times over.

7. **The Graham Family.** Kent's daughter by a previous marriage is **Bethany Graham**, married to **Jason Graham**, and mother to the rascally grandsons, **Gavin** and **Beckett**.

8. **Judith, Janie** and **Helen** are the kind of friends you can call at 3 in the morning and just talk. Judith and our mutual friend **Roger** have been friends since high school. Janie and Helen are two of the infamous Roomies from college days.

9. **Figaro** is a one-eyed, twenty-pound tuxedo cat. Possibly the best creature, in his weight class, on the planet.

10. **The WA Clownfish Asylum**, also known as **water aerobics**. My source of fun, exercise, and affordable therapy.

I just realized that except for the obvious exceptions of grandchildren, great grandchildren, and Figaro, this is a book about old people.

2020

It looks so innocuous, doesn't it? Nicely balanced. Two twos and two zeroes. One fifth of the way through a new century. I thought I would be reflecting to the beginning of this new century remembering Y2K issues. Would planes be able to fly safely? What would happen to our bank accounts? Would computers crash? And it was nothing. Just another day. Oh, we were full of anxiety for the coming of 2000. But 2020 was a sleeper. Holy moly. Were we ever unprepared. Trump was impeached in December of 2019 but acquitted by the senate in February, 2020. He remains the President of the United States. That alone would have brought me to my knees. But I did not have time for that to happen. A pandemic hit the planet, and that appalling leadership in Washington has proven daily how dreadful the intersection of his administration with a serious health threat can be.

The United States is now quarantined by the rest of the world. Please, America, stay home. Keep your absurd refusal to cooperate with people who want to prevent your illness and possible death to yourselves. We have become example #1 of what happens when "rugged individualism" becomes stubborn self-destruction. We do not have enough hospitals, enough PPE, enough masks, enough medical staff at every level. We do not have enough morgues, enough cemeteries, enough storage for bodies. The plague is everywhere around us. But because it is invisible, it is given little respect. Even as adults, we need our monsters to be visible and hiding under beds; a monster needs a human face apparently. When did our imaginations become so limited?

But the greatest of our insufficiencies is unity. In past decades, past generations, when an evil attacked our country, we put away our differences and came together as one determined and united people. It has been one of our greatest strengths. During World War II, our military was unprepared for the attack on Pearl Harbor. We were isolationists. We did not have munitions rolling off assembly lines. Our military was segregated. We were as unprepared as a country can be, inherently racist, as divided about the war in Europe as can be. But after that attack, we were one big fighting machine. Men enlisted. Men of every race. Women took jobs they had never done before. Women of every race. Factories learned to turn out munitions. And we hunkered down with ration cards and snail mail for years.

Where is America? Where are those never-say-die people who know how to sacrifice, endure, cooperate? When did we become so back-biting, hostile to one another, so ill-informed? Yes, the people sewing masks, the medical staff risking their lives and their families' lives, the people applauding their efforts each night, the sonnets online, actors and singers contributing their talent to amuse and entertain us are wonderful. They seem a drop into the bucket of boiling hate that has become our beautiful country.

People attack the very medical staff who work themselves to exhaustion for us. Wearing a mask that covers your nose and mouth to keep contagion from spreading is tantamount to spitting on the Bill of Rights. Tantrums, confrontations, refusals, fights, name calling, enemies made and acknowledged over wearing masks. Masks! We don't have ration cards. Snail mail has been replaced by Zoom connecting us with sound and pictures night and day.

Yes, the economy is tanking because our ability to work the way we always have, to earn money the way we did has been obstructed. There is huge unemployment, and employment has been our link to health insurance. Terrifying. It took a pandemic for people to realize how nearsighted that connection is.

But we have had to change the ways we worked in the past. We need to be innovative. Creative. We put a man on the moon. We stopped other diseases in their tracks. We are Americans. We figure it out. What is this national sniveling? Sure, we liked restaurants and bars, diners, getting together to break bread. Find another way to do it. It is not the sharing of food that is dangerous; it is proximity to other people. Of course, it doesn't feel the same. That is the point. It is a trade-off. Entertain yourselves and others in a new way or die. Surely, we can do this. If we cannot, 2020 will be the year that lives in infamy.

Abortion

Here's a difficult subject. While we are kicking and crunching in the water aerobics pool, we talk. Many of us have known one another for years and feel very comfortable talking about absolutely anything with one another. We do not all agree on anything except perhaps how much we adore water aerobics and especially the community that has grown up around water aerobics. We can agree to disagree.

This morning, we had someone new to the class, and we enthusiastically welcomed her. As we circled round our instructor for high kicks and warming up our inner thighs, the subject of abortion came up. I don't quite remember how. Some just listened. Others chimed in about the horror of carrying a child who resulted from rape to full-term. Our newbie was horrified. "The Bible speaks to this," she incorrectly noted. We apologized for causing her discomfort. She was in a rage. "You need to apologize to God!" she snarled and left the class.

It does seem to me that there are nine months when a woman's life, her body, her importance as a human being takes second place to grow an embryo and fetus. Once the baby is born, she reverts to that creature left out of the Constitution but at least permitted to vote by amendment. Statistics show that a large majority of people believe that our abortion laws should be left as they are under *Roe v. Wade*, with viability being the touchstone.

This move to revert to the bad old days is, in fact, the movement of a minority of our citizens. It would be even a smaller number if there were no women like our newbie who did not support the right to choose over their own bodies, their daughter's bodies. This minority is mostly motivated by religion.

I remember thinking that, once the genie of women's rights had been let out of the bottle, no amount of legislation or court rule would put it back in. Wrong again. And as usual, I am mostly astonished NOT at the men who want to put a cork in our bottle, but at the women who join them against their own best interests. Astonishing. Women convinced by other women that men have a right to make decisions about our bodies.

Are there any laws about a man's body? Can any man have a vasectomy without the approval of others? Is he not withholding a potential child's right to be born? Why do men have the right to govern their own bodies and women are denied the same rights?

Time travel has not been invented yet, but I suppose with a bit more effort, we can bring back the times before *Roe, 1973*. We can reverse civil rights, the right to privacy, we can reverse the right for people to marry whom they choose, bring back segregation, we can make people of color property, not allow women to vote. Who in this life wants to go backward? White men. And Clarence Thomas.

The Agenda

The other shoe finally dropped yesterday. We knew it was coming. It had been forecast for years, and then there was the unprecedented leak of a draft of the *Dobbs* case out of Mississippi. *Roe v. Wade* would be overturned. The reasoning, which any first-year law student could oppose, in the majority opinion was not surprising. What shook me to my core was Clarence Thomas's concurring opinion which no other justice joined.

You need to know that a concurring opinion is never required. It is often used when a judge joins a majority that seems contrary to his or her usual holdings for a special reason. A death penalty case joined by someone who may not usually support the death penalty because of factors that made the crime more heinous, for example. They often offer insight into the personality and thinking of the concurring judge and any others who join the concurrence.

You will recall that nominees for the position of justice or judge go to enormous lengths not to answer how they may rule on a particular issue that might be heard before them. Bias is the worst form of judicial corruption. It goes to the very heart of fairness. Smart nominees say that they will decide each case on the facts and law before them at the time. Suppose you are a dad in a divorce case and want custody of your child. If your judge believes every child should be raised by its mother, you will never get a fair hearing.

Thomas's concurrence is an excellent example of how not to write a concurrence. Instead of merely saying why he is voting to overturn *Roe*, he makes it clear that he is eager for cases to come before him that permit him to overturn gay marriage, gay rights and protections. This is not judicial restraint. This is not even judicial activism. This is an *agenda*. Judges do not have agendas. That is the entire point of a judicial system. One case at a time, apply the facts of the case to the laws in place at the time. Then another case. Then another one. The legislature and the executive branches have agendas. Thomas is soliciting cases to be filed and all but promising his vote.

Thomas has planted his flag on the marble arch. The timing could not be more informative. His wife and he have come to the attention of the committee investigating the January 6th insurrection. My mind has always found it problematic that Ginny Thomas worked for a political party, any political party, while her husband was on the Supreme Court. She did more than that; he was supportive. At the very least. A justice can recuse himself from a case if he feels that someone, a litigant, may perceive that the justice has an interest in the case. On the Supreme Court, a justice decides for himself if he should recuse himself.

Dobbs is a giant of a case, and it has underscored the cracks in our society and in a once well-respected Supreme Court. I refer you to the excellent article in VOX by Zack Beauchamp.

Aging

Later this week, I will be seventy-five. At least chronologically. Parts of me have been replaced. I have a hip that is about six and a knee that is about five years old. My lenses in my eyes are about five years old, too. At what point do the number of your replaced parts make you officially a cyborg? And do their ages somehow affect the age of the overall whole being. And that number would have to be offset by those parts of me that seem to be aging in dog years. My feet have significant neuropathy, and my hands have acquired a subtle shudder that makes my already sketchy handwriting indecipherable, even to me. But it is the loss of my brain that scares me the most. Our brains are the essence, the pith and nut of who we are. And mine has to stop and remember how to get to places that are very familiar. Names. Names of things, names of people, names of restaurants. This affliction is called anomia. It means you are losing, or have lost, your nouns. So right now, sitting at this keyboard, I can recall the noun "anomia" but keep forgetting the name of one of my favorite restaurants, "Lucilla". For no reason I can articulate, I keep calling it "Nutella".

I am a senior mentor for first year med students through a program at FSU's College of Medicine. They are studying gerontology, and the term "senior mentor" is what they call us volunteers. The term "Exhibit A" was already taken. They asked me last week to tell them how being my age was better than being in my twenties. I laughed. This was their attempt to put a positive spin on that aging process in which you lose your libido, your metabolism, and your memory. In trade for that I get _____. Right. After deep thought, I do not have to put up with periods or hot flashes.

My whole life, I wanted to be smarter, talented, pretty, accomplished. I looked at those gifted people around me, and I wanted to be them. To really excel, to win the prizes, the kudos. I worked very hard. I studied. I pushed myself. And now I cannot remember it and am just grateful for the life I have. Life. I have LIFE. It is the birthday gift I get each time I wake up to another day.

Ahhhhhhh

I can read again. Not just magazine articles. I can read books again. My attention span and focus have slowly emerged from under the bed where they were hiding from the wicked ogre in the White House. Whole days go by where I forget to listen to the news. My blood pressure has returned to normal. I watched Biden deliver his speech and thought: *This man is no orator, in fact, he is boring. I love boring. I love our new President.*

I was so moved by his genuine from-the-heart sincerity that, by the end of his unexceptional speech, I had tears in my eyes. He is just an old man trying to do the right thing. And I know he won't get everything right. But so far, I approve of his immediate attention to the deaths from Covid, the Asian killings, lowering the flag at the White House to signal his sympathy and shared loss. Once again, we have a mensch as our leader. He never stops working! He took on a raging pandemic, economic repercussions, white supremacists, plus all the usual backstabbing, underhanded folderol that passes as politics. He should be enjoying a retirement somewhere, writing his memoirs.

He was no one's first choice because he was, well, boring. He was not Pete, Bernie, Amy or Elizabeth who all burned bright. Too brightly to sell. Too new in one way or another. But he was the most centrist, the most saleable of all the Democratic candidates, the safest, and the others got behind him. He was vanilla after years of rocky road.

I worry about him, about his health, his stamina. The presidency is no cake walk ever. Not in the best of years. If you take it seriously [I never thought I would type those words], it is killing pressure and responsibility. He is no kid. And I worry about what will happen if he dies in office. We are so fragile right now. Our democracy is in tatters. We are barely keeping it together. But we are. And each day that goes by, we are closer to healing. But it will take years. Domestic, home-grown, home-fertilized, and home-nurtured terrorism is our biggest challenge. We need his practical, pragmatic self to continue for at least the four years of his term.

I wish Joe Biden well in every sense of the word. Let him live long, let him live strong and vital. He has our country on the oxygen of a good man trying to do good things. Heal us, Joe.

Alternative Lives

I am fascinated by the idea of parallel lives. Not reincarnation, serial rebirth, but the idea that there are other simultaneous planes of existence, alternative to the one we are all living here in Tallahassee, Florida. I am about as spiritually flatfooted as a person can be. I am talking science fiction here.

I tried asking friends from high school if they ever wondered about alternative lives. Did they ever wonder about being one of a big family, or being a different race, or marrying a different person? Their answers were that they wanted no life in which they did not wind up exactly where they are now. This seems to me a total failure of imagination. And also, a bit smug. But I did not say that of course.

I made a lot of hard decisions in my life. The decision not to have children was one of them. In some parallel life, did I have children? Was I any good at it? Am I happy as a mother? Are my children happy? Was I able to become a lawyer while raising children? Or did the idea of practicing law never cross my mind? Would I be a grandmother now? Both of my brothers are grandfathers now.

What if I am a man in an alternative life? Would I have gone to the Naval Academy like my father? Would I too have chosen a military life? Would I have married? Had children?

Or what if in another life I am gifted in math and science? The doors that would have opened for me! In this life, I took basic math so many times, I thought they would name the building after me.

Or what if in an alternative life, I die at aged five from falling down the stairs and into a tiny brook not far from our house. Cracked my head open. In this life, doctors and medication kept me alive. And a car came along, found me, and took me home all covered in blood.

"What if" looms large in my life. I am happy in my life, but the lines that play out from various options keep me constantly wondering: What ripples would that make? What if I did this differently? What I crave, of course, is some sign from the cosmos that in some simultaneous, parallel life, I made the right decisions. That all the mistakes I made in this life never happened in some other life. Isn't that what an imagination is for? Imagining what is on the other side of the hedge, around the corner? What could I be?

Or would that perfection not be satisfying, but merely boring.

Amaryllis

Since nobody put me in charge, I am declaring this The Year of the Amaryllis. They are just stunning this year. They are in bloom in many of the oldest gardens all over town. The older ones are all a deep red. But they have been hybridized to doubles, salmons, white, peppermint striped, outlined in white, and my mom's favorite: Apple Blossom.

Whenever my parents visited from Maryland, she and I would go to Tallahassee Nurseries. We told Gene Ellis, the original owner, that he should charge admission. Devoted gardeners that we are, we had visited nurseries all over this country. There was not one we thought could hold a candle to Gene's garden-cum-nursery.

It was there that Mom fell in love with Apple Blossom amaryllis. Gene was selling the giant bulbs from the boxes they had arrived in at the nursery. Each had a picture of the bulb in bloom. I think she bought the entire box. For me. It was a major point of connection for Mom and me, our love of gardening and flowers. Whatever other issues we may have had from time to time, we each loved one another's gardens and sent plants from catalogs to one another often. I could not grow peonies here. So, I sent peonies to Mom who planted them in her garden. And she loved their color, their fragrance. But not the way the Japanese beetles and ants were attracted to them.

When we downsized ten years ago, I brought many of my plants with me. Well, what I could. The Apple Blossom amaryllis were all planted in the ground. Still, I had many amaryllis, quite a collection. Some grow in pots here; some I have planted in the ground. This week, they are nothing less than glorious. Their huge stamens and pistils flaunt themselves, "Come and get me! Take me; make me your own." Little sex fiends. Their weakness is that they are top heavy, and rain will scar their petals and cause the whole stem to break with its brilliant cargo dumped in the dirt. But this week, it is perfect for them. Ma Nature got the weather and the blooming to synchronize just right.

Somewhere, people hybridize flowers to make them into new colors, new combinations, more disease resistance, taller or shorter, more drought tolerant, more sun tolerant. This is a job! People get paid to do this! Why did I never think about botany when I was oh, five or six decades younger? It never crossed my mind. But maybe if I had done that as a job, I would not love it so much. The perversity of at least this human brain being what it is.

I think, parenthetically, that there is also a job for me in the naming of things. Naming of flowers, "Bengal Tiger" is my new canna, and the job of naming lipsticks and nail polishes "I'm Not Really a Waitress Red", "Cherries in the Snow", "Boogie Beige", "Blue Note". My new roses are "Peach Drift". My mother and I both loved words, and I am half convinced that her love of "Apple Blossom" amaryllis was encouraged by her love for the song, "It's Cherry Pink and Apple Blossom White", popular when I was a child. It was associative and romantic. That was my mom all over.

My fraught love for my mom is blooming in the Florida sunshine. She is gone many years now, but the amaryllis we both loved, the flowers, the names of the flowers, their fragrance and resilience are all there to remind me of her. Happy Year of the Amaryllis, good people. We all awoke on the right side of the grass this morning. Let's celebrate.

Amazon

Wish fulfillment. Sounds like a job for fairy godmothers. Something out of a fairytale. You go to your computer, a magic wand if ever there was one, add to cart, and the next day, there it is sitting just outside your front door. That special cat food your puss needs? They have it. Keurig single coffee cups? By the gross. Books! Books to read to my youngest grandchildren, books to inspire my older grandchildren. Books for me and everyone I love. And stuff I did not know I needed until I saw it on Amazon.

I do not know how we would have navigated last year's unforeseen needs. Masks, then the right masks. Purell for our hands, rubber gloves. Amazon had it and got it to us ASAP. Responding to the country's needs it prioritized shipments of PPE. They felt more like an ally in the fight against the virus than simply a merchant.

And Amazon and Mr. Bezos made a lot of money. I do not begrudge them a dime of it.

My niece is appalled that I not only use Amazon, I sing its praises high and low. She says they don't treat their workers well enough. They pay the lowest worker at least $15 per hour. That is about double minimum wage in most states. They are against unions [duh], and their breaks are not long enough. They are work, people, during a pandemic that not only stayed open but hired on more people. They are not perfect, I am sure. But I sure love Amazon, the way they deal with dissatisfied customers, packages gone astray, the ease of use, their politics. Right, politics. Trump hates Bezos. That alone is enough to get you five stars in my book.

Mr. Bezos invented not the mousetrap but the better mousetrap. And indeed, the world has beat a path to his door. Jeff Bezos changed the shopping world. If you have internet service, you can get merchandise from all over the world. It doesn't matter if you live in Two Egg but want Manhattan style.

Two things have made self-isolating during the pandemic endurable: The first thing is all our electronic gadgets that have helped us stay connected. The second thing is Amazon. Thank you, Mr. Bezos.

And Another One Bites the Dust

We were visiting Israel so Harry could meet with colleagues and deliver a lecture or two. It was cold, and the two of us were exploring Tel Aviv on foot, as we did everywhere we went, looking into this shop, that gallery. Poking along with no particular itinerary. Some free time for ourselves was rare. These trips were work for Harry, not tourism. We were taking full advantage of this small window of time.

I have always loved glass. The way the light moves in the glass is a lover embracing a long-lost love. Movement and nuance, change of colors, glass and light together are magical. We happened upon a small shop selling glass arts. When we entered, there were two older men who spoke to us in Hebrew. Harry answered in Yiddish, because neither of us speaks Hebrew. Their faces lit up, and they both moved to embrace us. Yiddish does that. It is the mama-loshen, the mother tongue for Jews all over the world.

Harry had asked in Denmark, Germany, Israel, Russia, "Do you speak Yiddish?" Or simply said, "We speak Yiddish," and, in every case, —even Denmark! —we received an affirmative reply and an embrace. It is about two strangers in a strange land encountering one another and realizing they do not have to be strangers anymore. They speak the same language in every sense of that phrase. Landsman! Fellow traveler.

I take an aside here. Michael Chabon, the contemporary novelist, tells at the end of his novel "The Yiddish Policeman's

Union" how he came to imagine a novel where Jews had been given the right to settle in Alaska for several years. He describes happening onto a sidewalk sale selling phrasebooks for travelers. You could ask where the luggage claim was located, passport control, schedules in French, Italian, German. One of the travel books was in Yiddish. Where in the world was one going to need to speak Yiddish? It is not now, nor was it ever, the national language of any state. It is mama-loshen. The language of the home. He bought it, and he got to imagining a place to use the book. Alaska. Of course.

The men in the glass shop were brothers, both had numerals tattooed on their forearms. Harry explained where we lived, how we came to be in Tel Aviv on a cold night in March. They asked me questions, and I replied in the best Yiddish I could muster. At my house, it was the language my parents resorted to after we kids all learned to spell. My comprehension is better than my fluency, but I found I could stumble through it, and they were amazingly kind.

The brothers showed us every inch of their tiny shop, clearly bursting with pride. They showed us how they blew some things and compressed others. I fell in love with a large, heavy piece of glass about the size of a card table. We bought it, and the brothers agreed to ship it to us. But it wasn't enough. They wanted us to take more. Not buy it, take it. We tried to say no, but they also included three large platters, each different and unique, of about eighteen inches square. I loved them, especially one with alternating squares of orange and turquoise.

The huge wooden box arrived a couple of months after we returned from our trip. I used the card table sized piece of glass as a tabletop. I still do. It is on our porch where the glass and the light can enjoy their lovers' dalliance every day. Sadly, two of the big plates broke years ago when I stupidly washed them in water that was too hot. I cried. The third one was also broken, cracked, and for years, I just put it on display to enjoy the light show.

Last night, Figaro decided to sleep next to the last plate on display. In jumping down, he knocked it off balance, and it crashed to the tile floor, shattering into so many pieces, every person in the diaspora could have a shard. It was an accident. Figs is not destructive. I should have intervened. Moved the plate. Moved the cat. Paid attention to what was happening. It was totally my fault. Nothing lasts.

Harry is dead nineteen years, and I am sure the Israeli brothers are long deceased, too. Yiddish is a dying language. It was once the language of stories, theater, everyday life. Newspapers were published in Yiddish. I and the table on the porch remain. So far. We are both showing signs of wear.

Covid Chronicles 1: 3/27/20

I had not planned on dying the summer of 2020. So, when a novel virus reared its ugly head in January, my husband and I found ourselves glued to the TV. Coming soon to a neighborhood near you. It is coming. *It is coming.*

We listened, we read articles about the virus itself and how to stay safe. The more we read, the more vulnerable we felt. Emerging first in China, epidemiologists warned us: "It *is* coming to the U.S.." There is no vaccine against this virus and no medicine if you "catch" it. It is highly contagious. If you are a senior, it is more likely to be deadly.

Hospitals and morgues were overwhelmed as it spread across Asia and Europe. And people suggested that seniors should be ready to die to keep the economy healthy for their grandchildren. I felt like some low-on-the-food-chain prey, hiding out in my burrow, venturing out only to find food. And here I remain.

I am not ready to die. I have a few architectural issues, replaced joints, but am otherwise in good health. Same for my husband. We want to see our grandchildren graduate from high school. Hell, we want to see our grandchildren! And my much-adored brother and sister-in-law, and our friends: the movie-goers, the book readers, the foodies, the OLLI folks, my water aerobics buddies.

Every single hour, day, week, month we stay huddled in our burrows is another bit of our lives diminished. I read, and I write, and I cook and work with my orchids. I had hoped that for the first time, I'd enter one in the orchid show competition in April. But that probably will not happen now.

One looks for something good in every dark scenario. The ordinary people who arise from the corn to spread their altruism among those who are desperate for food and shelter. They are everywhere, contributing their own safety, their time, their compassion. They are nameless and will never receive the overwhelming thanks they deserve. They feed the medical personnel who are on the front lines. They are the glue in our society.

When I despair that our country has turned into something I cannot recognize, divided, hateful, xenophobic, I will remember these good, good people who were there, are there when the chips are down. We have true heroes among us, doctoring us at risk to their own lives, and heroes making it possible for the docs, nurses, medical workers to show up and do their jobs. I know throughout France, and right here in Atlanta, people are applauding you as you change shifts. I join them. I applaud those Americans who quietly take their place at the front lines so we can live.

FSU is a main draw — a remainder for no may friends to come to Tallahassee

And So I Came to Tallahassee

Way back in 1963, I did not know anyone whose parents were taking them to visit potential colleges. *What are they doing?* I wondered. *Counting the bricks?* I had always assumed I would go to college, took college prep classes, and at the end of my senior year, it was time to apply. Where to apply?

My father was very candid about this: "Listen, Paula Sue, I have sons to educate. You don't need to go to college."

My mother weighed in and said, "How will she ever meet someone to marry?"

I was aghast at this but kept my big mouth shut. I wanted to go to college. "If you can get into a Florida school as an in-state student, you can go there. Period." That was my dad's edict.

There were two state schools in Florida at that time: Florida and Florida State. My dad said Gainesville had no airport, Tallahassee did, and he did not want to be shlepping up and back, taking me to school. I wrote to FSU and explained that I had no home state. My father was career military, and we moved all the time. But he had been born and raised in Miami and admitted to the Naval Academy by the good graces [and doing very well on an exam] of a senator from Florida.

They wrote back immediately that I was welcome to come to the state of Florida as an in-state student. For the rest of my undergraduate career, my father referred to this as "Paula's flimflam". I have no idea why. I made my parents promise one thing: I would not have to change schools. If I went to FSU, I would graduate from FSU. No more moving.

And so it was that I found myself a suitcase and trunk that had belonged to my mother when she went off to college, my mother and maternal grandmother entering Tallahassee by Thomasville Road. "Well," Mom said. "This is it."

This is it? Really? I get to live here? Do you remember Thomasville Road in the early sixties? It was breathtaking! Huge trees sheltered a two-lane road. There were wildflowers blooming on the sides of the road, and Spanish moss hung from the trees. I was smitten. What a beautiful little town. And the campus! It was August 1963, and I was going to college.

It was hotter than hell, and absolutely nothing was air conditioned. Not the dorms, and not the classrooms. Not the cars. The heat and humidity settled over Tallahassee like a huge broody hen. Probably the corduroy skirts and sweaters I'd brought were not going to be practical for some time. But surely by September...

There were rules about what we could wear and what we could not wear. There were times we could go out and times we had to be in our dorms. This was all laid out for the women in a booklet called "Knowledge for College". The boys had no rules. The women had to pass a test on the rules before they could stay out past 8:30 at night. You could only wear shorts on campus if you were going to or returning from a physical education class. And then you had to wear a raincoat over the shorts.

What heat? The required dress code was a skirt or dress, every day, with pantyhose [just invented] or bobby sox [which no one would be caught dead in]. And of course, we wore slips because we were nice girls, and nice girls wore slips. Especially if you did not come from Florida and did not know that one more layer of clothes was not what you wanted in the heat.

On Saturday you could wear slacks, not jeans, unless you were going to the library and then you had to wear a skirt. Football games were attended in heels, stockings, Jackie Kennedy suits, gloves and a dead flower pinned to your chest. People fainted from the heat. There were bleachers we had to climb in those heels and narrow skirts. The football pantheon had not yet been built.

I loved every single second of it. I had not been singled out for the heat or the silly rules. We were all in this together. And what really made me happy were the other girls/women in the dorm. The dorm itself was one of the original women's college halls, Reynolds, and had not had a restoration or update ever. My roommate was a psychopath who used to call the dorm and ask to speak to herself to see if we would turn her in for staying out all night. No one ever did. But as the only two Jewish girls, of course we were assigned to room together as my housemother explained.

But across the hall were Janie Wells and Helen Murray, and to the other side, Sandy White. Janie and Helen were born and bred Florida girls. Sandy's dad had been teaching at FSU's extension center in Panama. The four of us became The Roomies, and we did everything stupid and everything smart together for the next four years. We lived together, had our first apartments together our senior year, fell in love, experimented with sex, helped one another, wore one another's clothes. After studying, we would walk to HoJo's on Tennessee Street and treat ourselves to bowls of clam chowder. We ordered pizza from Chanelo's, and Janie taught us all to eat our fried chicken with honey. Helen taught me how to eat raw oysters. We would sit on the stoop of our second-floor apartment and watch the sunsets. We were a quartet. I loved them then; I love them now.

When we graduated, we just kind of scattered, each into her own life. I exchanged a couple of letters with Janie, saw Helen and her family at least once, but from 1968 to about 2002, we did not have contact. Thirty-four years. Then that fate that brought us together as girls brought us together again. I was still in Tallahassee, working. My husband had just died, and Janie saw the obituary in the paper. She and her husband had retired to a little island off Wakulla. Helen and her husband had bought a house and retired to Mariana. No one had heard a single word from Sandy, and none of our efforts to find her ever worked. Helen, Janie and I, however, met monthly for the next seventeen years. We spent the day together, usually at my house in Tallahassee, but we also went to Helen's and Janie's homes. There was no hesitancy among us. The conversation and the time flew by. And I was amazed that after all those years, we were perfectly aligned in all that really matters in life. We shared books, listened to music from the 60's, celebrated our birthdays, talked politics, raged together, and we worried about our families together, discussing those things that could only be revealed to the most trusted of friends. I was with The Roomies strolling through art in the park four years after my late husband's death when Kent popped his head around a painting and said, "Paula, I was so sorry to hear about Harry's death." The Roomies came to our wedding. And we laughed. Dear God, we laughed until tears flowed down our cheeks. We often said our monthly day together was better than the best therapy. It felt like a six-week vacation. I looked forward to our gatherings, longed for them.

Then, in 2018, Janie died of cancer. It is her story to tell, so I will not tell it. But it broke this leathery old heart. Shredded it. I miss her every day. And until Covid-19 made it impossible, Helen and I continued our monthly days together. We have probably had our last Roomies Day. She and her husband are restoring a home across the street from their daughter in north Georgia, not far from Atlanta. But we had seventeen more years together than we ever anticipated! More than four times as much time as we had as kids. I am so grateful for every single moment with them.

And their coming to FSU in 1963 was as willy-nilly as mine was. A watershed moment in our lives decided in Janie's case, because her mother said, "Get in the car; you are going to college. Period."

Helen had been to FSU for some tennis camp and liked it. And I was here because Tallahassee had an airport. On such gossamer strands are the best moments of our lives forever entangled.

I have several degrees from Florida State. Chosen in the most superfluous way, it has given me more than any alumni association can ever imagine. I am so grateful for the learning, for the fun, for the sisterhood that passes for friendship. And that is how I came to live in Tallahassee.

And So It Goes

Just because we have been brought to our knees by a virus that has killed almost 200,000 people in the U.S. so far does not mean that the rest of the plagues have been suspended. In speaking with some younger people, I was asked if there are other things I worry about. Our entire west coast is in flames. Millions of acres are burning out of control. I fear for the people, the wildlife, the irreplaceable beauty. Most of the fires are from lightning strikes in tinder dry landscapes. The east coast has had earthquakes and storms of enormous ferocity and number. As I type, long, tall Sally has entered the Gulf of Mexico with destruction on her mind. The meteorologists at first said that Sal wouldn't even get strong enough to be a named storm. Just one more tropical depression looking to lighten its load on our coasts. But we don't really do little storms any more. Sally is depressed no more. She is expected to hit as a Cat 2 hurricane now. Although she could get tougher, meaner, more deadly before she lands. What climate change indeed.

And the flu shots are in. You remember the flu? It is still expected to hit with its usual ferocity this winter. We are reminded: "Get vaccinated." One good byproduct of the pandemic? If you are wearing a mask, social distancing, washing your hands, you are less likely to get the flu. Or many other transmittable diseases. It's a good thing.

Our children and teachers are struggling with all of the above while trying to wring an education out of an education system asked, once again, to do something that is NOT an education issue. Teachers have looked for lice, served breakfast and lunch, lectured on stranger danger and wearing a condom. They have been turned into social workers who also are masters of several academic subjects. Now their job is to keep the economy from totally crashing. Although they were probably not in the room when these children were conceived, it was expected that both biological parents could go off to work and leave their children at schools. They are every child's third parent. That they have children of their own, and parents, is neither here nor there. Like our medical staff, they are on the frontlines but with little or no PPE. Have you ever taught little kids? There is never a time when at least one does not have a runny nose, a fever, not toilet trained. The teacher deals with this. And comforts the child. So, mom and dad can work. The greatest problem with after-school care is getting parents to pick their children up when the program is over. Teachers are the keystone to our lives.

Our country is a hair's breadth from civil war. I am dreading the election and the aftermath. I honestly fear for the continuation of a country I have loved with all my heart for most of my life. I am a child who came to some cognitive understanding of what we were and what we could be in the sixties. I believed in us. I believed in goodness and right. I believed in education and science and technology. I believed in the great American experiment of democracy. I believed in our three branches of shared responsibility and action. I am perhaps the original true believer. I am aghast at what we have become. Who turned all these rocks over without concern for what might crawl out? I am heartbroken.

Dr. Fauci is the last public person I trust. Poor man. Dedicate your entire life to selfless public service and get kicked in the teeth for it. People don't like experts? Ignorance and hunches are as good as science, experience and intellectual insight? Sure, everyone gets something wrong once in a while. But look at his batting average. This is the captain of our team. Team Survival. He gets a salary. He is not elected. He has no reason to lie. None. He says look to late 2021. He can't factor in a civil war, of course. Or how vaccines can be delivered if our infrastructure is destroyed by storms, fires, earthquakes.

To the Horsemen of the Apocalypse, I bring a body that has turned against me and a brain that I can no longer really rely on. I have to find a way to make some kind of peace with all this. Do you think carrots and sugar cubes will help?

Another Fall

I retired without a single plan for what I wanted to do in my retirement. I was exhausted from my work life and needed a vacation badly. But when you own the candy store, no candy gets made or sold if you are not there. I had not had a vacation in many, many years. I had worked fulltime and had parents and a very ill husband who needed any "spare" time I had. I was not interested in building a mountain cabin, a beach house, or sailing off into any sunsets. I wanted to just sit home, read things that had nothing to do with my profession, and take each day, each hour as it came. We downsized to half the house we had and zero lot line for minimum outdoor maintenance. Lovely.

If you work for yourself, you cannot just pick a convenient day and say, "I quit." Cases have their own internal timeline, and I had to work on them until they reached their natural stopping point. But the day finally came when the last case closed. I was finished.

My weight was out of control, and I needed to put myself on my own priority list. A friend invited me to attend a 7AM water aerobics class. I had never even heard of water aerobics, but I was hooked immediately. It didn't hurt that as I was climbing out of the water at the end of class, one of the people in the class said, "Don't give up. Keep coming." Encouragement from a total stranger. I liked this group a lot. I gradually realized that this group met daily, rain or shine. At

7AM. I liked the challenge. I had always been a morning person in any case. I was in.

Two other things I had never heard of claimed some of my time. I am a senior mentor for first year medical students studying geriatrics and gerontology. Every fall, two 1-MED students are assigned to me, and it has been one of the most meaningful things I do. They want to know my story, my medical history, and what I want in a doctor. I tell them. They have given me hope that, even during a pandemic, we are attracting some of the brightest and best to medical school. And old people will not be novel to them.

OLLI stands for Osher Life-Long learning Institute. Sort of college for seniors. All the classes you wanted to take but had no room for in your schedule. No tests, no papers, just insights and facts from instructors who clearly love their subjects. It is infectious in the best possible way. I leave wanting to know more. I have learned about the Abrahamic religions, the Civil War, the Odyssey, the Iliad, Ovid, mummies, shrunken heads, Churchill, Bollywood movies, the Romance Novel, World War 2, World War 1, the music of Paul Simon, Early Rock & Roll, the movies of Nora Ephron and more. Excellent classes. My classmates are so smart. They make the classes wonderful.

And finally, I have time to do this: sit at my keyboard and just pound out whatever is in my mind. Memories. Rants. Times when I am just trying to understand something. I try very hard not to censor myself. [But I do try not to aggravate my brother.] Otherwise, I just sit down, and I suddenly remember Jazzberry, a dog I owned for almost twenty years. Smart, funny, a leader of the pack. Or I remember the smell of wet wool and sweaty third graders that permeated the cloak room where I went to third grade. Cloak rooms. Ancient history. Where do modern schools stash snowsuits, scarves, boots, mittens, gloves, hats, jackets, coats? Do little children still wear snowsuits? Do they still immediately have to go to the bathroom the minute that getting them into full outside regalia is accomplished?

My year still starts in autumn. Olli and the medical school start in the fall, and water aerobics does a fall shift in schedule when so many of our lifeguards return to their own classes. Another truly joyous season of retirement. It remakes itself each day. Just the way I want it to.

Another Monday

It would be a nearly perfect day in my few square inches of the globe if my husband were still not in pandemic prison in a Holiday Inn in Athens, Greece. Quarantined. Some things you just cannot make up.

Luckily, I am an early riser, because Greece is seven hours ahead of us. As I'm feeding our beloved Figaro and preparing to leave for water aerobics, I sneak in a call to the prisoner. He is bored but coping. Tested positive today. [Insert poop emoji.]

My 7AM water aerobics class has moved to Levy Pool on Tharpe Street. We were at Trousdell which is, I think, the best of our pools. Trousdell is huge, heated, our star. Levy is the oldest of our pools and only open for a few days in the summer when the kids are not in school [it is right next to an elementary school], and even then, just a few hours on those days. But we get the entire pool to ourselves, including a deep middle [the pool is shaped like an elongated letter vee, with shallower ends, and a deep middle] and it is deliciously quiet. It is unbelievably noisy at Trousdell. The pool, Trousdell, is right against John Knox Road and filled with teams practicing, swimming laps, yelling instructions, enjoying the water. We have Levy all to ourselves. It was a salve today. The water was perfect, the sky filled with leftover dawn clouds, and birdsong. No one had been in that water yet. No one else was there but the guards. It felt like being pampered.

That deep middle is wonderful. At Trousdell we are always in shallow water, too shallow if you are tall to really allow the water to stretch your vertebrae. At Levy, you can do your entire workout in the deep if you prefer. I do, thank you. Oh, it feels fantastic. The water is an anti-gravity machine, and your every bone and joint relax and let the water do the heavy lifting.

There were eighteen of us, and I was delighted to see two grandmother/granddaughters sets among us. How is this for unlikely? Both girls were halves of boy/girl twins.

My poor husband can only look out his window at planes departing for the U.S. and his wife and cat who want him home. In the meantime, though, I'm going swimming.

Another Trip Around the Sun

It is my birthday on Tuesday. No, not today. Tuesday. Although as my wonderful cousins insist, "Celebrate early and often." They are so wise.

Sharing my birthday with election day means that for most of my adulthood, I have asked for a big Democratic win as a birthday gift. This year, maybe more than ever before, I want a huge blue wave to rise from unexpected places washing red from the political landscape and covering the country's earth with a deep blue, gentle sea.

Steve Bannon, out of jail for his contempt conviction, while his attorney's appeal says that once the Republicans are back in charge, he is coming for Dr. Fauci and his children. A cleansing of deep blue would wash this monster away. Also, his creator. And that dreadful Roger Stone. Retribution and chaos are their weapons of choice. The lie, large and small, their daily scripture.

The news informs me that the people who were suddenly flown from Texas to Cape Cod using taxpayer money have filed a class action suit against Ron DeSantis. His wife's political ad is very affecting. If only he were that same person with other people.

There is nothing special about this particular birthday. But I feel the whole world teetering on some terrible, irretrievable brink.

If you are thinking of gifts and the election is outside your means, I also would love the Ukraine to prevail in their David and Goliath fight with Putin, and for Israel to remember who they are and strive to be their better angels. World peace is a size that fits all and can gleefully be regifted.

And so, another trip around the sun begins.

Aphasia

I was a teacher of the deaf for many years before I went to law school. Deafness is not an obvious handicap on several levels. It doesn't show, of course. But more significantly, the real core of the problem of being born deaf is that one does not automatically acquire language.

People would often say to me, "Well, why don't they just write everything?" Writing presupposes language. In the same way that most Americans cannot speak or write Swahili because they have never heard it—we are, in essence, deaf to any language we have never heard—American children born deaf do not know English because they have never heard it.

Language does two things: it gives us the mechanical engine for thought. That is received language. Further it is, at the same time, the vehicle for transporting that thought, transporting all knowledge, all culture—all information—to another human being. That is expressed language. To be without language is worse than being stranded in a strange land. At least in that instance, you have your own language, the one you acquired so effortlessly, in acquiring the syntax and subtlety, the order, of your native tongue with each breath of infancy. You have a framework, your received language. And you have all the information you have learned throughout your life, because information is conveyed in language. You are lingual. You are verbal.

This is in contrast to being literate which is language at an even greater remove. You know what language is and what it does on a fundamental, basic level. Your internal thoughts, your internal language give you a prompt with which to learn another language. But to be totally without language, to be without the concept of ordering thoughts, ordering words is to be stranded even within yourself, without words to help place your own emotions, your own thoughts in context. It was my job to give deaf children language.

Then, fifteen years after leaving teaching, fate threw me a curve ball. My husband had a stroke that left him globally aphasic. This means he could neither express himself, nor could he receive language. Because he was brain-damaged, language was no longer processed, ordered, in his brain. But unlike a deaf child, he knows what language is. His brain just could not process in-coming language or his desired speech. He was stranded, isolated from the world of communication and unable to give voice to his own thoughts. He was, in a sense, deaf to his own language.

His children were convinced that this was something I could cure. Cure his aphasia. Find a new place in his brain to store that language. And while you are at it, part the Red Sea and get pigs to fly. Let me admit here what I have never admitted before—I do not know of one person with damage to the language areas of the brain as extensive as Harry's ever to be "cured" of aphasia. Not one.

But this was my brilliant husband. He was a polyglot, full professor in organic chemistry. Writer of hundreds of scientific papers. We could do it. For years we tried "sign language," speech therapy, "total communication." We practiced phonemes, words and phrases. We memorized dialogues I wrote just for him, and vocabulary that pertained most particularly to him. And finally, I can report that Aphasia is the land where no one speaks the language.

The Art of Lying

My parents had creative minds. That is how I choose to look at it now. For one thing, they made up words for things. Many parents make up words for anything of a sexual or eliminatory nature. One of the things teachers of preschool ask is what the family words are for these actions for obvious reasons. You need a Rosetta Stone. We had those. But additionally, my parents called the heel of a loaf of bread the "crychik". It was most valued, and no one I have ever met knows this word. My parents had a word for the quilted silk-topped comforter they had for their bed. It was the "paranee". No other quilts, comforters, or blankets had that name. After several embarrassing incidents in school, my brothers and I figured out that we just needed to keep our mouths shut because we were apparently speaking a patois that no one outside the immediate family knew.

[handwritten annotation: One of parents did a ver poppy show]

Then there is what I can only call my dad's twisted sense of humor. I do not like onions. I have disliked onions my entire life. Also, I was apparently a very picky eater and did not like my foods to touch one another. Lots of kids go through this stage. No big deal. My brother and I LOVED frozen chicken pot pies, the little individual ones. My dad came home from work one day to find Larry and me working our way through one of our favorite dinners. "Paula Sue," he said, "did you know there are onions in there?"

I looked immediately to my mother for corroboration. "What?!"

"There are not," she said. "Ben, stop it."

Dad picked up the disposable box. "See," he said. "It says monosodium glutamate."

"That is not onions," my mother and I chimed.

"Oh," Dad went on, "they just call it that so people won't know there are onions in the pie."

My mother coolly said, "Listen to me, Paula Sue. I am telling you the truth. Monosodium glutamate is a seasoning."

I didn't believe a word she said. "Mom? Crychik? Paranee? The other stuff you made up because you thought we were too young? And how about only trashy women wear half-slips? How about you cannot go swimming for at least an hour after you eat unless what you eat is tuna fish. Then you can swim immediately."

I stopped eating chicken pot pie. My father thinks this is hilarious until one night we are at the dinner table, and Larry and I each want the last piece of chicken. You know, I lie to Larry, "That isn't really chicken; it is duck." I get the last piece of chicken. Larry would not touch it.

My mother gave Dad the evil eye and said, "See what you have done?"

Here we have an unintended contest as to which parent was least trustworthy. When we were all in college, we were playing Facts in Five, a sort of precursor to Trivial Pursuit with our parents. My mother loved all things musical and knew arcane things like the identity of certain sopranos. She answered a question correctly, but none of us believed her. She turned to Dad. "You know this name; we bought a record of hers."

"No," my dad said with a smile. Her correct answer was denied by the group. Do I even have to tell you the kind of hell that broke lose in my competitive family? I do not care if the Kennedys played flag football. Try Facts in Five with Ben and Gerry Levitt.

My parents died more than a decade ago, but their idea of making things up just because it was fun to outsmart your trusting children lives on. They each told us anecdotes about their families. Some are true, some are not even close to true. When we do our family Zoom once a month, I hear from cousins what they know about those stories. As a family, we piece together the truth. Geez, we think it is the truth.

I gave my dad this framed Brian Andreas piece for Father's Day long ago:

> *"I used to believe my father about everything*
> *but then I had children*
> *myself and now I see*
> *how much stuff you*
> *make up just to*
> *keep yourself from*
> *going crazy."*

August 2022

Covid in its latest mutation is more survivable if you have had your vaccinations and follow-up boosters. New boosters for those of us in the most vulnerable category because of age and other infirmities is supposed to be available by next month. I have not heard boo about it in weeks. When immunization became available for the very youngest of us, mothers did not line up with their infants. The top ten states have immunized 4.5% of infants under five years. In the bottom ten states it is about 1%. Polio has been diagnosed again.

The FBI, with a search warrant approved by a judge, supported by an affidavit, removed twenty boxes of documents from former President Trump's home. There were Top Secret and other materials that were not to leave the White House recovered. These documents had been requested previously. It was denied that they were at his home. I do not recall how many lies have been attributed to Trump, but here is another one. His rabid fanbase called for the FBI to be disbanded.

Our governor wants people with no education and no training in how to teach others to be hired as teachers. They just must be military veterans or first responders. It is hard to measure just how soul-crushing this is for the professional teachers. They are underpaid, told what not to teach, what books not to read, and told that anyone can replace them. I find it amazing that thousands of them still showed up for the first day of school and intend to teach the young lives entrusted to them.

They develop their own plans in case there is a shooting at their school because neither the state nor federal government will protect them. They have always been heroes to me, but this grim determination to be there for the citizens of our mutual future is just astounding. We don't protect them, we don't pay them, we think anyone can do their job. They persist. Singers, actors, talented, well-paid, and well-recognized performers win the Presidential Freedom Medal. Right here, in our local schools are the real heroes.

This is what I call the vanishing constitutional right to privacy. If you are an embryo or fetus of any gender, your right to inhabit a womb trumps the rights of the woman who provides the womb. If you are a woman of child-bearing age, you have no right to decide the most intimate decisions about your own body. At birth, the rights of little girls to decide their most personal decisions about their own bodies disappears. They had rights in the womb, but not outside the womb. When they are ten years old and raped, the resulting pregnancy is more important than their own lives. You might think that only men could have decided this preposterous outcome. No. Without the enthusiastic support of many, many, many women, this would not be possible. Women abandoning women. Slaves owning slaves.

Next week, our votes will be counted. It has never mattered more who you decide to support. I am going to vote Democrat. I am going to vote for teachers and vote for women. I am going to vote for the truth. I am going to vote for diversity, for equality before the law. Join me.

August 5, 1943

If they were alive, my parents would be celebrating their seventy-seventh anniversary today. My mind does this "alternative universe" thing where it follows several scenarios down their individual rabbit holes. My mother died of liver disease, and because the liver could no longer remove toxins from her system, she was often hallucinating, often frightened. Snakes [she had a deep terror of snakes] were crawling up the walls of the hospital. "Can snakes do that?" she would ask? We would assure her they could not. That she was safe. But the terror lingered in her eyes.

At the same time my mom was dying, my father began his decline. It would not be diagnosed until after my mother's death, but he died of MSA, Multiple Systems Atrophy. When they most needed one another, each was locked into a deep, black neurological soundproof room where they could not really hear one another.

My mother confided to me, "Your father mumbles all the time, so I cannot understand him. He does it on purpose. He's going to run away with this woman he met when he was twenty-one years old. In Switzerland."

Dad countered, "She says things that are not real words. How am I supposed to understand her?"

And each told me they missed the other. Although they were living together. In the home they stubbornly refused to leave for better caregiving and nurture. And I missed them both. My smart, well-educated, opinionated, funny, irascible parents were present physically. But just not there. Dad wanted Mom to cook. Mom wanted Dad to bloody well get it himself. My Dad was a coffee-holic but could not remember how to use the Mr. Coffee. My mother reasonably replied, "He knows how to make a cup of coffee." No. I don't want to go down this rabbit hole at all. Been there, done that. And I know the outcome of this hopeless scenario.

A different scenario though would be they are both quite elderly, Mom 95, Dad 97, but in good mental and physical health. They are still stubbornly dug into their home in Maryland, although none of their family lives within hundreds of miles of them. They would have pictures of all their great-grandchildren on the walls. I can go two ways here: pandemic or no pandemic. The pandemic would have isolated us. They would not have understood why we were not visiting. Why there would not be a huge family Thanksgiving. This would make mom cry. No. Not taking this turn either.

Healthy and no-pandemic it is then. Total fiction. Only now, I see my parents upset because both of their remaining children and all of their four grandchildren married out of our faith and culture. No. No need to go this way either.

I suppose accepting reality is the way I have to go then. Sheesh. Perhaps they were spared the pain of seeing their beloved family taking choices that they cannot accept or understand. And I cannot imagine having to try and explain the current world as it is to them. I cannot explain it to myself.

Happy Anniversary, Mom and Dad! I think I'll just remember all the times we all celebrated you two. You had so many wonderful years together. So much love, achievement, laughter. And I cherish those memories.

Covid Chronicles 2: 3/28/20

Buried alive, also known as social-distancing, finds me digging my way out of our comfortable hobbit hole. Size makes neatness imperative in a hobbit hole. Things that I had put off because I had a zillion other things to do instead – and almost anything qualified as a distractor – had allowed my master closet to become something slightly less than masterful.

Kent's side is neat. Dress pants, then those many pocketed everyday pants I call "custodian chic". Then shorts. And his shirts hung above all this. He does have the Fred Archives stored in there, too. The Freds are friends from the time they all went to elementary school together. None of them is named Fred. They thought this was hilarious.

My side is a paean to black slacks/jeans/pants. And many colorful tops. All arranged by color, and that is neatly done. But I have had a many decades' obsession for scarves. Big ones that loop around you, and tiny ones that look like something out of the fifties that barely make it around my neck. I have scarves that belonged to my mother and grandmother and scarves I have bought in my travels. I am often gifted scarves by family because, no matter how fat I get, they always fit. I have them stored in several large baskets on the shelves. This is not a good plan because I get it into my head that only a particular scarf will do for the outfit I am currently wearing. And I have to locate it in all those scarves in all those baskets. I am not neat or careful about this, and at the moment, my side of the closet looks like a bomb exploded in a scarf factory. BUT, and this is a Corona Crisis pledge: it shall be accomplished, and we will be on our lock down in a neater place. Surely you have noticed that Dr. Birx is also a devotee of scarves. Brains and style. They are soft jewelry.

I am not the only one using some of our cloistered time to clean and reorder. This time of year, it is tradition for those who would normally be celebrating Seder to clean their kitchens from top to bottom, throwing away those things that are not eaten during Passover. And spring cleaning is in the lexicon of everyone, from hobbits to apartment dwellers to those with homes as generously sized as their acreage. And I admit that I love the fact that, despite our intentional distancing, I am still connected to that tradition of women [mostly] stretching back thousands of years. Well, no Purell. Cleanliness may or may not be next to godliness, but it is our only weapon against Corvid 19. In a way, I'm just maintaining the armory.

Ballerina

For Norma

My dad was a home movie devotee. At his death, it was the home movies that had chronicled our life as a family that we all wanted. The problem was they were extremely flammable and would burst into flames. We lost a precious film of me dancing in the kitchen at our home in Virginia. I am dressed in my prom dress, and my high school sweetheart is dressed in his white formal coat. The happiness is beaming out of me. It burst into flames on the projector and is no more.

Saved from that fate is my career as a ballerina. You know how some children are just born with grace and muscle control? I was not one of them. In fact, for my five-year-old's recital I danced with one foot bandaged because really it made no perceptible difference in my dancing ability. I had stepped on a fish bone that afternoon at the beach, and it went all the way through my foot.

Tap lessons, too. Movie of the ever talented and graceful Paula Levitt going through her moves, huge grin on her face, on the family porch. My skinny legs are pumping away in time to music heard only by me. Whenever we watched that reel, everyone, most especially me, would laugh. It is as if I emerged from the womb an ungainly, but happy mess.

When we were in middle school, junior high school, Larry and I started dancing together. We had discovered *American Bandstand*, and there were some moves we needed to practice. We got especially good at the cha cha and later even won some prizes at the O Club [Officer's Club]. We would practice in the kitchen to whatever came on the radio, and sometimes Mom and Dad would ask us to dance for them in the living room. And Dad would be there with his camera, saving our youth on film.

Dad spliced some films together with shots of signs he made with the date or an explanation of what we were seeing. But other films were only marked with some writing on the outside of the box that contained the film. Sometimes just a date. Where were we? Who are all these old friends now strangers?

I took the entire box of films down and had them converted to DVD's. Sadly, they could not be previewed so we could put them in some kind of chronological order. We could not risk another flash fire. I had copies made, and in all these years, I have never watched all of them. It made quite a few DVD's, and I find it deeply sad to see so many of my family who are now dead. There they are young, vital, funny, loving and silly with no thought of what life will hold for them. But I want you to know, that there exists a record on film of how that skinny legged ballerina learned to dance.

Bangs

For Betty Matousek

Betty posted a PSA that if you are going through a rough time, do not cut your bangs. Immediately, I had this memory of a four- or five-year-old Paula waiting impatiently for her mother. It was a very hot, sticky summer day in Brunswick, Georgia.

My dedicated mother, who had only been my mother for that short time, did not yet know how totally hopeless dance lessons were for me. There I was sticking up out of the crowd of little cuties, the onion in the petunia patch. With a bit of burnishing, surely this lump of coal would reveal the diamond my mom was sure lurked deep within me. She still had hope. She had allowed my thin, shiny hair to grow past my shoulders, and, yes, I had little girl bangs. Mom was really trying.

It was so hot. I had been trying my hardest in dance class, and I was hot and sticky. On the way into our house, Mom was waylaid by a neighbor who wanted to discuss gladiolas. Again and again, I tried to get my mom to come in and get this hot hair off my skinny shoulders. She turned around and said, "Paula Sue, you are being rude. I will be there in a few minutes."

My mom's dresser had a big mirror and was full of all kinds of mysteries. Cosmetics, mostly lipsticks in bright reds, and ah, yes, there they were, manicure scissors. They are tiny, of course. Child-sized. I couldn't make a ponytail by myself, but I could banish that hot, hot hair.

Snip, snip, a thousand little cuts as close to the scalp as I could get it, my shiny hair covering the floor and top of Mom's dresser. When it felt cooler, I stopped. I went outside and presented myself to my mother who was horrified. I never saw a picture of myself with this self-inflicted style, but it made my mother cry. Making your mother cry is one of the worst things a little kid can do. The guilt is overwhelming, and I cried too. Not because I was ugly without a single redeeming feature, but because I had made my mother cry. My mother picked up her hand mirror and showed me myself. "See what you have done?"

"I was hot," I wailed.

I cannot prove it, but I wonder if enduring subsequent years and years of Toni home permanents was some subconscious payback on her part.

The Bathing Suit Brouhaha

I retired and started going to water aerobics classes in 2012. A friend went and invited me to try it. What a revelation! I don't know why I was so surprised; I have always just loved the water, but I was unprepared for the camaraderie, the sense of accomplishment, the plain old fun that I found at seven in the morning, six days a week.

I think this may be the best kept secret in Tallahassee. Men and women show up, irrespective of the weather, and greet one another warmly, do calisthenics in the water, or dance, or play a game our inventive instructors come up with. I am sure there are days our laughter can be heard for blocks.

These are all men and women of a certain age. Usually, an age north of sixty. Sometimes well north of sixty. And age, living, and gravity, genetic disposition, and the realities of solving loneliness and depression with ice cream are all there to see. Just like in every single other activity we enjoy.

We do not look like those lovely young people who wear spandex like a second skin and strut around with pelvic bones akimbo. Dear God, they are lovely. And, yes, they too come to the pool.

So, for eight years now, I have been a Water Aerobics missionary proselytizing the joy and deliverance of chlorine and sunshine. How many converts can I brag about? None. Not a single one. I have offered to drive people to the pool, to meet them there at times I do not normally swim. Nope. Not gonna happen.

Want to know why? It is because to swim, you must wear a bathing suit. The horror. I have been slim, and I have been fat. I prefer to be slim. Who doesn't? And as Cher [dear God, I'm quoting Cher] once said, "If it came in a bottle, everyone would be slim." It doesn't. And I am fat. My mother, grandmothers, and great-grandmother were all shaped exactly like me. I am apparently genetically prepared to face a Russian winter but find myself in Florida. Eating ice cream.

When I am slim, everyone says how much I look like my father. When I am fat, everyone says I am my mother's clone. But I am no fatter in my bathing suit than I am in anything else I wear. Do I look fat in my bathing suit? Of course, I do. That is reality. And I am fat when wearing jeans, when wearing a dress. I am the same weight when I garden, when I cook, when I read and when I show up at water aerobics. Nothing about a bathing suit makes you look different than you do any other time of the day in any other venue. And no one cares.

Oh, we all wish one another well, and if you are on a diet or a life-changing course of exercise and diet change, you will find lots of support among the people at the pool. But really, no one cares. There are so many other things in this life to worry about.

I am not going to let my weight keep me out of the water. The exercise is good for me. It will be good for you, too. Meet me at the pool. And, yes, we have to wear bathing suits.

A Beginner's Clay Animal

When I look at snakes and especially manatee, I think to myself, *God was just practicing when he made those.* He was a beginner God, and he was given a large lump of clay. "Start with a really simple shape," said his mom. "A nice long snake is a great way to start. Just roll that clay back and forth in your chubby little fingers and watch it elongate. You can make big ones and little ones. Coil them up and make them look ferocious. There you have it. Your first animal. Now let's try for something a tiny bit harder. Let's give it a wide, flat tail and a couple of fins. You can start by rolling the clay in your hands again, but this is a chunky animal. Husky. Make it all of a piece, not like some mammals which we will get to later that look as if the tail is stuck on in back as another appendage. No, for the manatee you want one continuous line all down the body. Gently flatten the end so it can flutter. Beauty is in the eye of the beholder. You are getting very good at this. Now go ahead, put their faces to yours and gently blow. Watch the tongue on that snake. Give them life. Give them movement."

"I see you have lots of parts left over. Some random tails and horns, some bills, webbed feet, stripes and dots. Let's not let anything go to waste. Musk oxen! They will be completely improbable. And let's make a platypus. We have made so many gorgeous animals, these will be just for grunts and giggles. Always try to leave room in your work for humor. You cannot expect mankind to completely fill that space. And try to keep him away from the other animals. He is not a team player."

"Blow gently now. Set them exactly where each should go and then stand back. It will not be for you to determine what happens next. They 'll know."

Birds

I have loved birds, all animals really, for my entire life. I once kept birds in cages, and then I had birds I allowed to fly around and come into their cages at their choosing. Now I can no longer stand the idea of anything in a cage. I cry at zoos. "Such a tender snowflake," you might laugh. But the thought of one creature removed from community, removed from mating, reproducing, their movements compelled by instincts buried deep in their DNA thwarted makes me so sad.

I cannot even come to grips with goldfish anymore, forever bumping into the glass of their bowls. Why are they incarcerated? Because they are so beautiful and we want to watch them. They are guilty of color and grace. Felony beauty. Locked away for a lifetime.

Is it in Genesis that man is given dominion over the animals? Did the animals get to vote? We grow them, change the way they look by directing their reproduction, we eat them, separate mother from child. We kill them with abandon, even to extinction. Research the safety of our cosmetics on their captive eyes. What a creature is man.

I cannot love, cannot even like a person who does not love an animal. When I traveled this globe, I measured each civilization by how it treated its animals. They are so vulnerable to our willingness to go after their paws and claws with high caliber guns. People are so much more dangerous than animals.

Lots of us anthropomorphize our pets. If that is what it takes to give them empathy, I'm all for it. What would it take for us to feel that empathy for one another? I have bird feeders in a couple of places in my miniscule yard. Most of the neighborhood does. The birds fly from feeder to feeder, finding their favorite seeds. I love watching them visit us. *What will it take*, I wonder, *to make sure our human neighbors have enough to eat?*

Birthdays

It is almost November, and that means that the Ben Levitt tribe is about to have a glut of frosting, melting candles, well intended gifts. All three of my parents' children were born in November. It is as if some genetic switch is thrown in February, and our reproductive systems scream "Spawn, spawn, spawn!" And so it is that we have children, grandchildren, and the occasional spouse born in the eleventh month.

My brothers and I nearly always celebrated our birthdays together. My middle brother, Larry, died twenty years ago, but when Marty and Beth moved to Tallahassee after Marty retired, we have reverted and celebrate together. Our birthdays are only eight years and six days apart.

I know that lots and lots of people have younger brothers that they adore. But I think I simply win the prize for the best all-around brother ever. His birthday was my lucky day. I remember it very clearly because Dad picked me up from school which was so rare that it may indeed have been the only time. Ever. He told Ms. Oblivious that she had a new brother and his name was Martin, we would call him Marty. He was so cute!

I was the built-in babysitter, nanny, overseer, and person responsible for Marty. Worked just fine for me. I was there when he pointed to the sky and said, "Look! Hopptyclipter!" I was there when he was learning to ride a trike and could only pedal the trike backwards. I was there when Alice, his beloved stuffed giraffe, had to be washed and dried and Marty had to be comforted that Alice would emerge warm and clean and safe. I was there when he dreamed there were giraffes under his crib and we all got down to look carefully to assure him it was not true. Not a single giraffe.

Important things Marty and I share: carrot cake is our favorite; ice cream is the perfect food (although anything with melty cheese is in the running); we both like to eat early; we adore our spouses and never hesitate to say so. We both think he is a great guitarist; we both love *Sea Shanties* and other records and music that reminds us of brunch at our mom's table. Brunch, huge creative brunches, are our favorite meals. We both love Thanksgiving. We both agree on politics and religion and most of the other things people think are important. Agree may be too strong a word. We accommodate one another's beliefs. We both love, love, love music.

My baby brother was elected to the American Philosophical Society, Ben Franklin's version of the Royal Society in Britain. I was there when he was inducted, wearing a huge campaign button that read "Marty Levitt's sister". I am insanely proud of him and all he has accomplished in his life, despite our dad never understanding exactly what Marty did for a living.

So, October, do your ghoul thing and then get out of the way. Here come the Levitts. Marty's birthday is November 2.

The Blessedly Common Cold

The "Big O", Omicron variant of Covid has one more thing to answer for: it has turned us all into hypochondriacs. My own cooking gave me indigestion, and the left side of my head is completely closed. I have a mild headache that will not go away, and all in all, I feel like—well, bad. But I have no fever, and tests indicate that it is not in fact Covid. NOT. Guess what, one can still get a plain old everyday cold and just need bed rest, Tylenol, and lots of tea. It may still be infectious, however, and swimming in forty-degree weather while wearing a mask and feeling like death warmed over is not as alluring as it once was.

One of my WA mates is just recovering from her second bout with Covid. She is triple vaccinated, but Covid just likes her. The first time, it went to her lungs, and I was really afraid we would lose her. But she is one tough cookie who has survived some horrors that left her scarred for life. This is no quitter. The second time, it gave her what she describes as a sinus headache from hell that lasted seventeen days. She still looked like someone recovering from something awful when she showed up for the first time a couple of days ago. She is as disciplined and as regular as an expensive timepiece; she comes to WA every single day and swims on Sundays. She loves the water, and though I never say this lightly, may love the pool even more than I do. Yet because of Covid, this was her first day in the pool in 2022. The last thing on the planet she needs is to be exposed to my cold. And what some might describe as "mild", she was not hospitalized, it was excruciating, exhausting. I do not want even a "mild" case, thank you.

I miss her and my other WA friends. I miss our bawdy laughter and foolery while we kick, twist, stretch. But a little more contagion is not needed. Only a few of us wear masks. I wish everyone would, but I cannot blame people their frustrations when three jabs later, we are still told to not only wear masks but to wear a special kind of mask. Who knows what is working and what isn't any more? But a sneeze, a cough, a mild headache can send you running for a Covid test. The fact that winter often visits with colds is forgotten. Is this ache from Susanne's tough workout, or is it something sinister?

Like everyone else in the world, I am beyond ready for all this self-examination to end. I want to go back to my life. I want to be among my friends for meals at restaurants. I want to eat someone else's cooking. Inside. I want to go to a brick-and-mortar bookstore and to Tallahassee Nurseries. I want out of my hobbit hole.

And then I remember the people of Tonga who were going about their quiet South Pacific lives when a volcano erupted, and their lives disappeared. They lived for thousands of years in a geographical hobbit hole, restricted by island living in a part of the world few even knew existed. One hundred seventy islands. About halfway between Hawaii and Australia. How's that for an address? Life's realities come flooding back to me. I have been in self-imposed lockdown for so long that I forget that there is a world of aggression, pain, tragedy out there. Are we going to war again? Get over your bellybutton gazing, hobbit girl. You miss bookstores and nurseries? Poor you. There is a whole world out there.

A Blood Sport

My parents were ferocious competitors. They had trophies for golf and bowling, and they played poker, bridge. Scrabble was a blood sport. They loved to watch televised sports together, each taking a different team to root for "to make it interesting". Well, except for the Army/Navy game. No one at our house was going to cheer for Army.

Playing games with them as a child was awful. I thought of games as what you do for fun. If you won, you were gracious about it and said something like, "I got lucky." If you lost, you were gracious about it and said, "wait 'til next time."

Not my parents. Every hand, every bid, every play was to be vivisected for where you went wrong, got fewer points for the team, disgraced the family name forever. I successfully avoided all family games and all sports. There was nothing but barbed wire in that field. Yikes.

I married a man twenty-two years my senior. He was born the same year as my father. He loved to play bridge, as did many of our friends. He promised we would not yell at one another or belittle one another over a game. No vivisections. I got a book, and Harry taught me how to play. Our friends could not be kinder. I loved it, and we played once a week with friends and taught our teenaged sons how to play. We had a lot of fun with it.

Then Harry became ill. Lots of things stopped on a dime. In the blink of an eye, in an unexpected instant, our lives changed.

Harry could not speak. But he wanted to continue playing a game that requires partners to communicate with one another. What could Harry not do? Communicate. He was globally aphasic. But if Harry wanted to play bridge, we gave it our all.

When I say our friends were wonderful, I mean it. I typed the names of the suits on a scrap of paper for him. When he would bid, he would point to the suits he wanted on the paper. Well, that was the theory. Sometimes he would say one suit and point to another. He would not always understand that he was giving us mixed signals when we tried to untangle what should have been a simple bid. Sometimes it worked, sometimes not. The last time we played, we were playing with our boys who were visiting. I think Harry bid no trump, but thought he had bid spades. When he tried to trump a card, he became furious. The frustration he lived with, day in and day out, gave him a very short fuse. This was supposed to be fun. It had been for years. But now it only underscored all we had lost, and all he lived with. His death-defying life was the real blood sport.

A Bloomin' Genius

I have always been quite tall for a girl/woman of my generation. I am 5' 9" tall [or was before I shrunk]. My nieces are taller than I am. But I have been this height since I was ten years old.

My parents took me to doctors to see if there was something wrong with me. My growth rate was astonishing for a few years but stopped at age ten. My first male teacher was my fifth-grade teacher. I was taller than he was; there it was confirmed in our class picture. My body was incredibly skinny, and I had nothing that passed for coordination. My body had to catch up to all that growth. Who put that foot way over there? I was essentially the female version of Baby Huey.

So, we would move to a new school and the principal or registrar or the nice lady at the desk would take one look at me and say, "How old is she?" with total disbelief. I was also always one of the youngest in my class because my mom may have cheated a little so I could start school and save her tattered sanity.

Then came the inevitable IQ test. It never occurred to anyone to ask if I ever had taken the test before. The answer, since first grade, would have been, "You betcha." Almost every year since first grade, I took that test. I discovered when I was in college that all those tests were carefully reported on "my permanent record". I got to see that because, in college, I worked in the registrar's office. And let me tell you, what I found made me laugh out loud. The first time I took it, I had a normal, completely unremarkable IQ. But every successive test after that, I just got smarter and smarter. I was a bloomin' genius! Let me tell you, the people who received my report cards and math grades knew very well that nothing could be further from the truth.

But my teachers saw those silly IQ scores and were dumbfounded at just how ordinary I was. Except in math. In math I was dumb. Clearly, I just was not trying hard enough. Not living up to my potential, a gap that was growing with every school.

When I got to college, I had to take a beginning math survey course. I worked my tush off, but as soon as we moved from one type of math to another, I forgot how to do the previous calculations. I just could not hold them in my head. I was so sure I could not pass the final that I withdrew from the class. I retook the class the next semester and again withdrew at finals time. I was terrified.

My instructor took me aside my third time through. I had him the previous two times, too; it was not his fault. "Just take the final. You can do this." Third time was the charm. I think they should have named the math building after me. My roommates never let me live this down. And it is all there on my permanent record. With my genius IQ.

Body Language

One of the things that I love most about retirement is being a senior mentor for first year med students. I think this is my tenth year. The medical school matches me with two young, bright, hard-working students, and I am "Exhibit A" in their study of gerontology. That's what the "senior" means in senior mentor. It means old. I am well-experienced in how it feels to have your body turn on you and your mind go walk-about.

Yesterday, I met this year's duo, and they were wonderful: young, ambitious, and eager to enter medicine, even with a pandemic raging just outside the door. Like everything this year, we "met" on Zoom. All other years, I had them to my home and plied them with coffee and cookies. Their professor gives them questions to ask us, and they have a kind of script they can follow if talking to a stranger is too awkward. These two were easy, and our conversation flowed. They used the prompts only to get the information they are supposed to uncover during their interview. They wanted past medical history, family history, a condensed version of my life's story.

And one of the questions they asked was what I wanted in a doctor. Great question, don't you think? I said I wanted a doctor who thought my life was as valuable and precious as I did. I did not want to be shuffled out with a "She's lived a good long life". I am not yet ready to die.

And I wanted someone who was fluent in body language. The body has a very limited vocabulary. It has rashes, fevers, coughs, sneezes, pain, cramps, headaches, vomiting, diarrhea, bleeding, and others. I would guess that there may be twenty or thirty symptoms in all that our body uses to tell us how we are. The same twenty or so symptoms combine and recombine just like in our spoken language. But with far fewer "words".

Ambiguity is deep in the process. There are the names of bones, body parts, and processes. But I would guess that a vocabulary of a thousand words is all we get to describe everything from allergies to zygotes. I want a doctor who is fluent in this difficult language. I want my doctor to translate this for me, fully, so I can make informed decisions. And a sense of humor would be nice.

Covid Chronicles 3: 3/31/20

Yesterday wasn't a good day at all. I awoke feeling totally disoriented and ghost-walked through my typical chores of feeding the cat and folding and putting away yesterday's laundry. Then I went out on the back porch with a cup of coffee and cried.

I felt even worse about my plight because I was whining and sniveling. But it was a deep depression, and I just couldn't shake it. No one wants to be the weenie who can't do it when all their friends have girded their mental loins and are coping. Not sniveling.

I tried to put my finger on exactly what was getting to me. Pretty sure the problem is that even prisoners in jail have a beginning and ending date for their sentence. Well, we sure don't have to worry about a beginning date, do we? The last time I was out for lunch or any other social gathering was March 13. It was Nonnie's birthday, and only two of us from book club showed up to celebrate with Nonnie. We are all in that extra vulnerable demographic; really, March 13 was pushing it. So, we did not share one dessert, and instead of lingering for hours, we wished Nonnie well and went home.

Kent's birthday was five days later, and we cancelled it. We have not had book club [I know about Zoom and Skype and these other wonderful techie things, but at our ages, not everyone knows how. We did not grow up with computers.]

Kent has not been to the gym; I have not been to a Water Aerobics class. We have not gone out for dinner, visited our grandchildren. I deeply miss family meals on Sundays with my brother and his wife. There will be no Seder for us this year, and my granddaughter who lives in New Jersey will not be travelling to Tallahassee this year.

I will not be cooking my gold-medal-nothing-like-it chicken liver pate this year. There will be no need for matzoh, brisket, macaroons. Why not just ream me out of all the things I love?

Okay, yes. My orchids, oblivious to my droopy face, are blooming their gorgeous heads off, and they have a long way to go. But will we have Thanksgiving this year? Can I attend my grandson's fifth birthday in July? His brother's birthday in late November? Will we all ride the Polar Express again this year? Pile Christmas into our car and drive to Central Florida?

Or do we have to wait for a vaccine? What do we look for as an end to this sentence? No new cases? Tests for all?

I have one of those old-fashioned calendar books that has a column for each day this year. It is filled with holidays I never knew existed. It has all the holidays I share and all the ones Kent and his family share. And I have looked through it carefully. There is no future date that says, "It Is Over."

I know when Buddha Day is; I don't know when I get my life back.

Bonus Child's Birthday

I have no biological children, but two marriages to exceptional fathers have netted me six, yes, six, bonus children. I hate the words stepmother or stepchild because they are just fraught with horrible connotations. When we marry, as I have said before, we get the whole mishpocheh, the whole clan: children, friends, aunts and uncles, cousins, first wives, you name it. In-laws, out-laws, best friends and old enemies. It is a wicked pyramid scheme.

Kent brought to our marriage his son, Ross, who graduated from high school about a week before we were to marry. Ross pronounced me too fat to marry. It was not the best beginning. Also sacrificed on the high altar of blended-family-attempts was his lovely daughter, Bethany, who has been unfailingly kind, civil, and inclusive. She has married and given us two grandsons that I adore and who exhaust me. She treats me like family, but better. She never forgets a Mothers' Day or my birthday. She has amazing energy to heart-rassle every day with her two little boys. She is a fulltime Mom, fulltime wife, fulltime sister, fulltime employed outside the house. She and her dad chat about three times a week. She keeps in touch with her mother's friends and family. She has quietly stepped up to fill her mom's shoes.

Bethany's mom died a few years ago. If I could give Bethany anything in the world, I would give her another hour with her mom while her mom was not sick. If only that were possible. We often do not take our parents' advice, but just to hear it, just to have the person you love most in the world consider your deepest issues is the greatest present ever. That is how it is with Bethany. I want the impossible for her. Nothing but her heart's desire will do. She so deserves it. Of course, I will have to settle for something of this world that can be wrapped.

I married my fat self to Kent on June 3, 2006. But I soon learned that this date, April 25, is as close to my heart as it can get. Happy birthday, lovely woman. You are cherished.

Book Report

I have had an unusually good run with the books I have been reading. They were so good that I decided I had to sit down and tell you about them. Every one of the books was chosen because I had read other books by these authors and loved them, for various reasons. And I found them converging in my brain.

Anthony Doerr wrote *All the Light We Cannot See*; it moved me enormously. A blind French girl and an impoverished German boy are caught up in World War II, each a pawn in life's bigger plans. War and hatred, being enemies is not the choice of either of them. I could not put it down. I was a bit disappointed in the ending, but it underscores how war so often elevates us to our best selves. The times after the war we revert to being ordinary.

This time, Doerr gives us *Cloud Cuckoo Land* which reaches back to one of the sieges of Constantinople and forward to future space travel. Again, children are his main characters, caught up in circumstances beyond their control. Whether in Constantinople in 1453 or The Lakeport Public Library in 2020 or aboard, The Argos on Mission Year 64, the children are struggling to understand and to stay alive. Their stories are the stories of innocents getting through each day.

Amor Towles wrote *A Gentleman in Moscow* and now gives us *The Lincoln Highway*. The elegance of *A Gentleman in Moscow* is now the humor of *The Lincoln Highway*.

This time, Towles took on writing a picaresque novel. Yes, that is spelled correctly. The first picaresque novel is thought to be *Lazarillo de Tormes*, a Spanish novel from about 1550. The protagonist is a young boy, a rascal, who travels through life getting himself into one trouble after another and always forgiving himself in a fact-shifting way. *Tom Sawyer* and *Huck Finn* are both picaresque novels. The protagonist of Towles's *The Lincoln Highway* is a lad named Duchess. In fact, the main characters in *Lincoln Highway*, just as in *Cloud Cuckoo Land* and *All the Light We Cannot See* are mainly youngsters. Billy Watson is only eight. The "big kids" are all waiting to turn eighteen and age out of Salina Reformatory. You can forgive youngsters a lot. Not everything, but a lot. More than you would forgive an adult. Oh, and Ulysses is one of the characters. The great Ulysses, not President Grant. Put aside some time for these novels. You will not want any one of these books to end.

Enjoy.

Born to Rumble

I think there is a Bruce Springsteen song in here somewhere. Why is America so contentious? I was lucky enough to attend a lecture by Supreme Court Justice Sandra Day O'Connor many years ago. She pointed out that our very founding documents anticipated dispute, dissent, litigation. Our Constitution is a majoritarian document appended by our Bill of Rights and amendments which are about individual rights. And this is not an accident. Many of those who agreed to the ratification of the Constitution did so only with the understanding that the Bill of Rights would quickly be forthcoming.

But look even earlier: we have this wonderfully hyperbolic language about We the people. We talk about "All men are created equal." Nearly every single founding father was a slave owner. There is promise, and then there is reality. What is a man? Not people of color, not women. Almost 250 years later, we are still hammering out the dissonance. Look within the Constitution. Look at what we civics class graduates call checks and balances. Legislation and acts of the executive can only be addressed by filing a lawsuit. Litigation. And I point out that only the Executive Branch has an army. We have to rely on citizens to follow the rulings of the courts. Tell me that isn't looking for trouble. Courts, too, can make mistakes.

Once while visiting in Japan, a man told me that America would never be great because we were so diverse. Not the word he used. I was a guest, a woman, and it is rude to disagree in Japan. I said nothing. But I believe, and I think most

Americans believe, that it is our very diversity that has made us who we are. Our founding fathers were white, Anglo-Saxon, protestants. WASPS. They were writing for themselves. And started a fight for equality that rages up to today. And in the meantime, we have accepted and been joined by citizens from all over this planet. Men and women of every nationality, ethnic origin, religion, political persuasion. We invite them in. They come seeking refuge and a better life. They are born here, and they are brought here. And God love us, every single one has a closet full of opinions firmly based on their experiences and their learnings. Two hundred and fifty years and Black Lives Matter is a contemporary and meaningful issue.

A new Vice President of the United States is chosen, and we are repeatedly reminded that she is not only the first woman to serve as Vice President, but the first African American and south Asian to serve in that capacity. Race and ethnicity are still news. Gender is still news! Half the population is female, and gender is still an issue.

Kamala Harris sees the world differently than I do. She must, because her experiences and learnings will be different. She will be joined by lots of WASP men, a few Jews, a few other women and men of color in Congress. There will be dissension, and there will be agreement. Feelings will be hurt, sometimes unintentionally. Often not.

When we say we are the Great American Experiment, this, I think, is what we mean. The people who think Democrats are a large pedophile ring, the people who stormed the Capital, the tree huggers, scientists, and vaccine avoiders all consider themselves patriots. They love this country. They all know very little about the Constitution, but more about their First Amendment rights of speech and assembly. And they intend to exercise them. They are ready to rumble. Bless their hearts.

So here we are, a big amalgam of unmatched values and needs. We are governed by a Constitution and other founding documents that are still looking for explication and their place two hundred and fifty years after they were drafted. By quill pens and ink. Into a world where indoor plumbing was not yet available. If we are still here, we are patriots. We think our country beautiful and our opportunity best here. Yet many are furious that their place in the constitutional sun is still not assured.

Japan cut itself off from the outside world for hundreds of years to find their homogeneity. Surely, enforced homogeneity is the very essence of racism. I could happily do without the anti-Semitism I have encountered in my life. I would like us all to find a way to live inside our bodies and give respect to all the different modes and variations bodies come in. Here, in America, I have hope, real hope, that we can do that. That we will. That I will be included in "We the people" and "All men are created equal".

Boutique Geri

I don't even know how this got started. I was living in Tallahassee, going to school, and my parents had moved twice since I had graduated. When my Roomies went home to visit with friends, attend weddings, go to parties and reunions, I stayed on campus. Not having a hometown, and then moving after graduation makes going "home" a lonely endeavor. So, I didn't. I was totally surprised when I did get to my parents' new home outside Buffalo, New York, to discover that my mother had started her own company, and it was going great guns. I was nothing short of astonished that Boutique Geri had been created out of her fertile brain and was up and running.

My mom was a very creative person. She took thirty-plus barely habitable places, turned them into a home, left them all better than when she found them. In the kitchen, she was amazing. We all bragged about her inventiveness and her good food. She could knit and was the queen of afghans and warm slipper socks. She was a nurturing gardener. But never had I seen her do anything like this. Whoa!

What Boutique Geri produced and sold were topiaries for the powder room that had vials of perfume [something good smelling] hidden deep within their foliage. The base was a small clay flowerpot that my dad had painted [possibly Marty helped here, too] in an array of vivid colors. The topiary was made of silk flowers of all kinds that my mom bought from some supplier in every hue you can imagine. She made every single one by hand, and each was unique. Dozens of them.

They were finished with gorgeous ribbon. They took time and an eye for color. And they were selling like hot cakes. Mom had a clear wrapping paper that went around each finished topiary with a gold sticker that said "Boutique Geri". They looked very professional. They had taken about a dozen to several of Buffalo's big department stores, cold called in most cases, and in every case, they were snapped up. She was understandably very proud of them, and during the visit, we went to several department stores to see them on display. I have never seen her so happy. Boutique Geri was her baby, and it was doing beautifully.

My parents lived for nine years in Buffalo. At that time, my dad was out of the Navy and working at Cornell Aeronautical Labs. He and Mom decided to move back to the Washington area so Dad could start his own company. And he announced that he would no longer help Mom with Boutique Geri. This, perhaps more than anything they had ever gone through together, broke her heart. Dad's company, Summit Research, was born, but Boutique Geri, my mom's company, was terminated.

He encouraged her to continue. But she was sure she could not do it without him, and Dad needed her to work in the company he put together. Everything about this last move made Boutique Geri impossible. Her suppliers of pots, silk flowers, her contacts at the department stores were all in the Buffalo area. She had moved all of their lives, again and again, and here she had created something out of nothing. But that was the end of Boutique Geri. For a while, some unused pots and silk flowers lingered around. But eventually the last remnants slowly disappeared.

The Navy almost certainly would not have allowed an officer's wife to have a cottage industry in her home. In Buffalo, they were no longer with the Navy, and Mom could strut her stuff. But Dad was the unchallenged leader and head of the family. It wasn't as if either he or Mom liked Buffalo. They hated it.

They much preferred the D.C. area where there were so many retired military. More people like them. And my mother was a very supportive and loving wife. If Dad wanted to start his own operations research company, my mother was going to be right by his side, cheering him on.

I know my dad worked late into each night to get his own company up and running. It was very successful, and that is because my mother and father both put their shoulders against that hard wheel of accomplishment. In many ways, it was *their* company. They succeeded beyond their dreams, I think. They were both proud of it. And I know it takes creativity of a certain kind to start any company, and operations research requires yet another kind of creativity.

But as an adult and wife of many years, I look back at all the many things my mom gave up to stand by her man, Levitts United. My parents were married for sixty years. Boutique Geri was the hardest loss. The equation for a long marriage has nothing to do with "fair".

Bridge

Something is interfering with my writing. It is a game that my late husband asked me to learn. Bridge. I think most young people do not play this game anymore. I did not want to learn how to play bridge because my parents were ferocious bridge players. It was a blood sport played around a card table. The way my parents played the game, there was a rerun of each hand pointing out bad bidding, bad play, and how if the other had only bid, played, lead differently, the game would have been theirs. Post-mortems. Even when they won, they did this. If you bid and made game, you should have made a grand slam. It was exhausting.

Recriminations and accusations do not make a fun game in my mind. But Harry swore he would never do that, so I ventured in and soon found I loved it. Before he got sick, I played at least weekly with him and good friends, or with girlfriends. That all stopped when he had his stroke, and many years went by when I never even picked up a deck of cards. On the very rare occasion that I played, I humiliated myself. I had forgotten so much.

Three friends, Margaret Lynn, Shirlee, and Jeanne insisted that my play would get better and would not let me quit. I apologized after every game for my inability to remember what had been played and by whom. Honestly, I cannot count the times I thought they would do so much better with a new fourth. But they persisted, as friends do.

Because we are friends of a certain age, we have learned to play online, safely in our own homes, on a platform Jeanne found for us. Trickster Bridge has become a thing with me and is eating up the time I once spent writing my deathless prose. Trickster offers about a dozen other card games, too. You can arrange a foursome as we do for bridge, or join a game already in progress in bridge and other games. No one around to play? Computers take those positions. Although I think the bots are idiots.

When I cannot sleep, I play bridge with total strangers and sometimes the occasional bot. As in anything that is essentially anonymous, there are some bad actors. The twits who have a void in hearts, for example, and bid six hearts. Then they run away from the board. Or the wiseacre who comments with emoji on each trick. On a good night, you find three real, reasonable, bridge players, and off you go. The hours zoom by, and I have discovered that the more I play, the more comfortable I feel. It is a kind of therapy.

Tomorrow, these three wonderful women who never give up on me have a game arranged for us at 12:30. They are so good. So generous. So kind. If I had sisters, they could not be as patient. I hope they can see I have been practicing. I am striving to get better.

But I'm Not Finished

Today is the last day of 2021. I still cannot bake a decent loaf of bread; I have not lost as much weight as I promised myself [someone has to eat all that unsatisfactory bread]; I have not cleaned out the garage; I have not written something I thought worthy of submitting for consideration of publication, well, one tiny 250-word bit of micro fiction; the pandemic rages on, and I really miss what we considered normality. I'd like a time machine to go back to 2016 and see if we can get it right. Biden has proved to be mortal, after all, and is dealing with a hard "no" from his own party about work he holds dear to his heart

On the other hand, my dead cells have been working overtime and show no sign of resigning. My hair has grown from wash and wear stubble-length to collar length. Donald Trump is not President of anything. He also is free as a bird, unindicted, his lawyers having appealed and appealed and appealed. Is there a statute of limitations on treason?

My ability to read has returned. I credit the fact that I seldom watch the news anymore, and Donald Trump is not President. My cringe reflex can relax a bit.

In about eleven hours, the planet will have completed its cycle round the sun, and a new year will commence. 2022. I am hard pressed to think of anything positive to say about 2021. That year cannot leave yet. It has been fires, pandemic and mutations, hurricanes, monster tornadoes, inflation, mass resignation, revert to feral behaviors. It seems the beginning of the end of democracy. It owes us something good. It cannot be just unabashedly grim. 2021 is a thug. It wears a perpetual sneer.

I come back to that one candle I hold aloft: Donald Trump is not President.

Butterscotch

But for the intervention of the men in my life, I would probably have about ten dogs and an equal number of cats. Restraint is not one of my qualities. I lead with my heart and then figure it out later.

Once I was driving down Tennessee Street on a hot summer morning. I realized at a stoplight that I was driving behind the dogcatcher. A beautiful wheaten terrier jailed in the back of the truck made profound eye contact with me, and I followed the truck to the pound. I asked if I could adopt her. Well, the pound said she had been picked up because her owner said she had dropsy, and they could only allow her to be adopted if she were healthy. I asked if my vet could examine her. Dropsy is fluid retention. My own more prosaic view was the dog was very pregnant.

I took her to my vet who said not only is she pregnant, but those pups will be coming fast. It is the vet who said she might be a Wheaten terrier. Who knows? He called the pound for me, and I took Butterscotch home, bathed her in warm water, which she loved, and get a big box ready for her.

I awoke the next day to what, at first, sounded like an animal crying in distress but was actually Butterscotch and her huge litter. I think she had seven pups by someone who was not a Wheaten terrier and left no forwarding address. She was enormously hungry, and while she ate, I looked at what a simple drive behind the dogcatcher had netted me. Both Butterscotch and I were in heaven.

I had a big fenced yard, and Butterscotch loved to run around in the grass with her brood chasing her, tripping over their own paws, being totally adorable. When they were two months old, I put a sign offering puppies at the laundromat and one on the bulletin board at the grocery store. My co-conspirator vet vaccinated them all and pronounced them all healthy and um, ugly. Well, they were healthy mutts. So, what. I sold each for $10 which pretty much covered vet costs and puppy kibble. I hope each landed in a good home.

Butterscotch and I settled down to a lovely life together. At the time, the home I was renting did not have air conditioning, and I often left windows open for a cross breeze. One day, some friends and I were playing bridge in the living room when we heard the most suggestive moans and groans coming from outside. Wow. Someone was having quite a time. Finally, we could not stand it and had to see what the blazes was going on. Those deep, sexy moans.

What we saw was Butterscotch under the hedge. She had found a low branch and was scratching her back in that devilish place none of us can ever quite reach. Her eyes were closed and she had a look of pure bliss on her face. One of my friends said she knew it had to be something like that. I looked at her. Liar! There was only one thing anyone could think listening to those moans, and it was only tangentially related to having your itch scratched.

Sadly, someone stole Butterscotch out of my locked yard while I was at work. I was heartbroken, and can only hope she landed in a soft, loving place. Surely Dante saved a special circle of hell for creeps who steal pets. Lowest of the low. Butterscotch: I missed her loyal companionship, her playful spirit, and those suggestive moans.

The Calm After the Storm

I am sleeping a little better; my midnight solitaire sessions are fewer. There are days I hardly think about politics. I can safely say I never wonder if Biden is about to do something irredeemable to our country. In fact, I basically don't think about our President at all, except to look at him as a fellow septuagenarian and think how hard the presidency is on anyone who steps into that role. I pray for his continued health. While I completely agree with those who say "get past it" is not appropriate for an attempted coup in which people died, I am hopeful that some federal prosecutor will take this out of the hands of the politicians entirely and indict the man for felony murder.

My blood pressure and anxiety levels are both about where they should be for an old, fat person living in a pandemic that keeps morphing and mutating faster than our vaccines can be delivered. Several of our friends have had Covid and somehow made it safely out the other side. Kent and I stay hunkered down in our hobbit hole. We have each had both shots, and maximum efficacy should kick in in about a week. This offers some to no protection against the fast-moving mutations, but it is better than having nothing at all. Mother Nature is kicking our collective butts, isn't she? Done in by an invisible enemy that can mutate around our defenses.

I keep trying to swim every day. For years, I went to a 7AM water aerobics class and started each day with hilarity, friendship, renewing movement. It does not exist now, and more than any other thing, what I miss the most is that class.

We had two or three different instructors in a week, and it was always changing, always something different. And at the best of times, we were squad. We would sometimes go for coffee or breakfast after class. In wet bathing suits and robes, we met at a McDonalds for unpretentious coffee and chat. We cared about one another's surgeries, setbacks, accomplishments, creativity. Women of a certain age going through the patch, patch, patch of our later years together. Now, if the temps fall below forty, I bring the orchids in, and I give myself the same care: no swimming in air colder than forty. So, I have missed a few days in the water this winter.

A couple of good things have emerged from this isolation: My extended family, cousins and their spouses, and offspring and their offspring do a monthly Zoom. I love it. We are spread across this continent and into England. Most often, we tell family stories, share photos, check in on one another. And on Saturday afternoons, I sometimes play a couple of hours of bridge online with friends who I played with for years around one another's tables. I keep telling myself that I'm going to study in between our games. But it doesn't happen. They are saints for putting up with me. And on Tuesdays, this same quartet gets on a conference call to chat, check on one another, touch base.

For twenty-five years, two friends from high school and I wrote to one another daily. Because I am in the East and they live in Arizona and Utah, I would start it, and each of them would reply all. About a year ago, we morphed to a weekly three-way phone call. Although I do love hearing their voices and laughter, I also liked the writing. I miss it. You write about things you may not so easily talk about. It was more intimate.

Soon there will be six weeks of OLLI classes. I have signed up for three. And while I enjoy them, they mean more screen time. More watching life go by inside a flat screen. Everything I do seems to require a computer, a keyboard, Zoomability.

Critical to my well-being are the Facebook friends who give me their opinions, agree or disagree with me, teach me, laugh with me, take the time to respond. What a gift you are during these times.

It will not be long until spring throws open its doors and windows, and everything begins to emerge all new for another year. I am longing for that time.

Cell Phones

I have consigned another cell phone to a watery death. May she rest in peace. It was not murder. It never is. No, I am the queen of negligence, and this no doubt why I never had any children. The fates knew I could not be trusted.

My first cell phone died in the bathroom of a museum in Philadelphia. It was a very nice bathroom. I did not want to put my purse on the floor, and there was no counter or hook on which to place the purse. So, I put it on the side of the sink and used the facilities on the far side of the room. As soon as I sat down and all my clothes were wrapped around my ankles like so many pythons, the contents of my purse shifted and the purse slid into the sink where the motion activated faucet turned on. The phone was drenched before I could lurch myself to its rescue. RIP first phone. No, rice did not do it. Nothing did it. I probably imagined the small scream of terror.

So, I bought another phone, she wrote as blithely as if these bloody things grew on trees. But they are required now, aren't they? And they store all our information which is why I often cannot remember anyone's phone number. And they have the word game where I am now at level 568. And it is the only way to get texts. So, I will live one less month in order to afford it. What the hell. I get a new cell phone. Until one night, I am lying in bed listening to the washing machine make strange clopping noises, and I race to the laundry room because my cell phone has gone to the place all good gadgets go riding in the pocket of my jeans. My recently laundered jeans. *Sigh.*

This is one of the very few times I wish I lived alone. I could hide my shame. I could just buy a replacement after I sell the family silver, and no one would be wiser. But no. I have a loving husband who does not even get angry at me! Rice? Too far gone.

Yesterday, I was just exhausted all day and went to bed grouchy and very early with a good book and fell asleep before the washing machine was turned on. You know that my third phone was in my jeans pocket, of course. You know I did not even realize my latest costly stupidity until my husband gently told me that he had heard it in the washer and rushed to save it. Too late.

If there is an afterlife for cell phones, I do hope it is dry and protected for them. Maybe they float on clouds of rice, just in case. I have no harsh feelings for them. I meant no harm to a single solitary one. But that makes three cell phone deaths on my head and on my conscience.

I will be sending out string and clean tin cans to all of you. Please shout. I'm getting old.

Cell Phones, the Sequel

In spite of my initial thought to send out hundreds of miles of string and a lot of tin cans, I spent yesterday at the AT&T Store, getting fitted with a new cell phone. One calls for an appointment, is masked, and sits at a table across from the tech person/saleswoman. We are further protected by a window of plastic. There are about ten customers in the store.

My dearly departed cellphone was five years old and entirely adequate to my geriatric needs. I have never used the garage band app it came with, for example. I never measured anything with the measuring app. I just want to communicate with people. I really don't even take very many pictures. That is my husband's bailiwick. I want Gmail, Facebook, and text. And a telephone. Oh, I also want Marco Polo because that is the app I use to communicate with my grandsons, aged three and five. So, I thought I'd just replace what I had.

They no longer make it, of course, and wasn't I just the cutest thing. Apparently, like dogs, cell phones age much faster than we mere mortals. I think they can choose a mate at about age two. This was an experienced sale person, however, and she figured out in ten seconds that if she told me she had a cell phone in red, she had a sale.

I am really not sure how much it cost. One cannot just walk in and pay for a cell phone. Don't be absurd. You have to dribble out $10 or $20 dollars a month, added to your plan, and added to your husband's cell phone costs but subtracted by AARP deductions and other specials. I think MIT has a course in how to make this calculation. Our salesperson spent quite some time scrolling through her sales tablet, looking for other specials and deductions for us. I spent that time gazing around a store that sized me up as totally out of my depth. Yup, I like the red one.

My savvy husband had come with a list of passwords we use for various sites: Google, iTunes, Facebook, Gmail, Amazon, Apple, AT&T, Google, iCloud. If my previous phone had not died, I could have just transferred everything from the old to the new. But alas.

No, I took home my shiny new toy, and Kent and I alternated screaming at inanimate objects as we tried to decipher exactly how to reload my phone. Let me say the restraint Kent has shown in not losing his patience, suffering my alternating fury and frustration all magnified by my guilt, should elevate him to the level of Mother Theresa who probably never laundered her cell phone even once. Kent has never done one in either. A fact he is way too smart to point out to me. If only the string and cans would have sufficed.

You are far smarter than I am. You check all the pockets of the clothes you are about to wash before you put them in water. May you achieve the Nirvana your enlightenment deserves. I am going straight to phone purgatory.

Covid Chronicles 4: A Pandemic Letter to Mom and Dad

Dear Mom and Dad,

You must think me strange to be writing to you so many years after your deaths. But you have been so much on my mind lately that I felt I simply had to sit down and do it. You will correctly think me absurdly sentimental, but I occasionally call your home telephone number. So, maybe a letter isn't that strange. I still feel attached, I guess.

The world is so unbelievably different from the one you knew. There are several things that are just staggering: climate change. The polar ice caps are melting. The seas are rising. Our entire geography and life on this planet are about to change.

In the election of 2016, Donald Trump was elected President. He did not win the popular vote, lost that by about 3.5 million to Hillary Clinton, but he won the electoral college. Either one of these issues will be the subject of dozens if not hundreds of books.

But now comes the real clinker: the world is in self-imposed quarantine of greater and lesser strictness because of a viral pandemic sweeping across the world. The virus is not one that the scientists knew anything about before this outbreak. It causes severe respiratory distress and pneumonia. There is no cure and no way to prevent it, no vaccine, so people are isolating themselves in hope that they can avoid the virus. We are told that they [the CDC and WHO, among others] believe that it is spread like a common cold, from effusions leaving one person by coughing and being inhaled by another. That is a very simplistic explanation. But the major point is we need to stay away from everyone except those we live with.

The hospitals are overflowing. New York City has been the hardest hit. The governor there is Cuomo, and he has earned the respect of all by the way he has handled an unprecedented crisis. Conference centers and temporary MASH type wards and hospitals are struggling with the overflow of sick people. Tents. People are being admitted to the hospital and placed in tents. There is not enough medical equipment and palliative drugs.

The medical staff is exhausted and are catching the virus themselves and sometimes dying. Obviously, there can be no visitors. The contagion possibility is too high. So, people who have to be admitted have to say goodbye to their families. If they die, they die alone. No family and friends are there for them. Families might not even be told of a death until days later.

The morgues are full, and bodies are being stored in huge refrigerator trucks. It is heart-breaking. The virus is most likely to be deadly in those with underlying illnesses like heart disease and diabetes, and the elderly.

Some of our friends are fortunate enough to still have living parents. You can see why, at this horrible time, you have been very much on my mind. I thought I could never think this, never write it down or express it, but I am glad you died before this horror.

Losing each of you was excruciating. But this isolation and dying alone is a whole exponential increase in grief and anguish. This pandemic has done the impossible: it has made me grateful that you are dead. Safely passed. What a world.

Chat

Went to see my family doctor last week for what I think of as a well-baby check-up. I had lost weight, my blood pressure was totally normal, and my cholesterol, dear people, was 170. Eat your heart out. I thought I'd get at least one attagirl, but no. *Sigh.*

There is always something. I feel like Roseanne Roseannadanna. I will be 76 in less than a week. I exercise six days a week. I have many of the issues that come with being old. I think of my mother and grandmothers and wonder what came floating in on my DNA when I was conceived. I can tell you that none of them was svelte. Not even close. And I often feel that I am swimming upstream, trying mightily to be the person my mirror wants me to be. Which genetically speaking I am not.

My mother died at 80, my maternal grandmother at 88, and my paternal grandmother in her 90's. They went to their graves with everything they were born with intact. No gall bladders removed, no hysterectomies. No replaced hips and knees. Other than osteoarthritis, everyone in my family aged without a huge amount of medical intervention. Well, both of my grandmothers were suspected to cheat at cards, but that is uncorroborated. It is what I want for myself, too.

When the doctor says some number is not what he wants to see, I want to change it with diet. I cannot reasonably do more exercise. I do not want to take meds. They always have side effects that are worse than whatever ailment I am trying to avoid or mitigate. I come from that era when the first birth control pills became available. They contained 10,000 mg of progestin and 150 mg of estrogen. I was on them for decades. The later birth control pills reduced the progestin to 50-150 mg and 20-50 mg of estrogen. The higher dosage I was prescribed increased the likelihood of heart attack. My first cardiologist refused to continue to treat me if I did not get off birth control completely. That was a long time ago. My point is that what is prescribed in one decade may be completely reversed in the next. So, I try not to be on medications. My grandmothers are examples of aging with the least possible medical intervention. It seems right to me.

My doctor deserves kudos for keeping me relatively mobile and healthy. I am not 50 or 60 anymore, and I can tell. The familial arthritis is having its way with me. My once absorbent brain has gone to hell in a breadbasket. One day, I will die in spite of everything they do. In spite of everything I do. I would love to live to 90, only if I can do it without enormous pain and without being a weight on my family. This getting old stuff is tricky.

Choosing to Be Happy

Good morning! Isn't it gorgeous outside? My love of life in Tallahassee often makes me wonder how people actually choose to live somewhere else. I have a good friend from high school who moved with his wife of fifty years to Park City, Utah. In their retirement. All that snow, ice, killing temperatures. They love it. He reminds me that I loved the snow when I was a kid and the fun we had playing in it. Seventeen is another planet from seventy-five. For me. Seventeen is just some bio-electrical charges in my faltering brain now. But I'm so glad they are happy and that not everyone wants to live in Tallahassee. I like this size. In fact, a bit smaller would be fine, too.

Last night, the weatherman advised that it would go down to thirty-four in the early morning hours. My loving husband and I then schlepped some fifty or sixty orchids inside. Again. If they gave frequent schlepping miles, we'd be rich. I am still deeply repentant for leaving them all out and the dreadful aftermath. I have been trimming dead parts, watching for signs of regeneration. Many are showing just how resilient they are. Others, not so much. I am not taking any chances. The problem with bringing them in, besides the sheer laboriousness of it, is that inevitably some struggling bloom spike or buds get knocked off. It aggravates the devil out of me. We try to be so careful. So right now, the garage and the house are filled with orchids. And probably tiny lizards and the occasional frog. Figs is on high alert.

Figs has brought us two voles in a single night. This is the true sign of spring. The voles had no voice in this being the chosen sign. Not bad for a cat who is blind in one eye. The happiness we draw from that cat, the warmth and silliness of him, his rounded corners bring us so much more than we could ever give him.

I often write about my memories and many people have been kind enough to remark how happy my life has been. How fortunate I have been. No one can reach my age and not have lost people they loved, still love, deeply. Life, being mortal, having every single thing around you subject to the randomness of the universe gives you two small choices: Absorb the pain and continue, or be undone and lose the chance for happiness now. I try mightily to choose happiness. I try to remember and put the best spin on my good memories. The ones that are too brutal will never be written, but I promise you, they are right there in the front of my brain. I hope you do not see this omission as a kind of deceit. It keeps the black dog from the door. I often think I am a better on paper than in person.

There is Figs and his voles, the promise of a birdsong-filled morning, there is the potential for an April filled with orchids in full bloom.

Happy Monday. Happy day. I choose happy.

Christmas

I, like most of the U.S., am about to celebrate a Christmas. I was born to a Jewish family, was raised sort of a bagel-and-lox secular Jew, and am married these last fifteen years to a Christian. My cousins are all Jewish, my whole family is Jewish, but Shirley says I am "barely" Jewish. This is not true. I am as Jewish as a secular person can be who has been raised not only among Christians but in places there just were no other Jews. All of this this epistolary tippy toeing gives me away, doesn't it? I feel a bit guilty about looking forward to having Kent's grandsons, their parents, his sister and her husband, and their grandchildren all join us in our hobbit hole on Christmas. We have our fake tree up, and it is lighted and decorated. It is surrounded by a train and wrapped gifts. There are stockings hanging at our faux fireplace. We have kissing Santa and Mrs. Claus salt and pepper shakers. My parents are whirling in their graves.

It will not reduce my Jewishness by so much as a nanogram to make my husband and his Christian family happy. I am delighted to do so. Gavin wants a turkey. I will roast a turkey. My husband wants mashed potatoes. Done. It looks like a re-run of Thanksgiving to me, but that's okay. I like Thanksgiving.

I love these people, and I want to make them happy. What worries me is that Kent's late wife, the "real" grandmother and mother of this crew, was a pedal to the metal holiday conjurer. I hope I do not disappoint them. I am sure their expectations are high. It is their favorite holiday. It is a bit tricky to navigate the line separating over-doing it and not doing enough.

And no one else at my Christmas table will know it, but it is also my late husband's birthday. I invented a holiday for him called Heshmas, and for thirty-two years, we sang the silly songs about him I wrote to Christmas tunes. We should be having either lamb chops or duck. His favorites. But he has been dead for twenty years. Except in my head.

I am trying very hard not to let my own expectations get away from me. My grandsons are five and six. They will be sleeping in a strange room. I am not sure what they expect, but we have tried to anticipate. They may have a too-much-sugar too-little-sleep meltdown. They will certainly scare Figaro the cat. Maybe they won't like their gifts.

This is just anxiety talking. I can do this. I think.

Cinnamon

It began as a bet, but the exact nature of the bet I cannot quite remember. I was a freshman in college. I think I had written a paper and thought I would get an A on the paper, and my friend and biggest critic, Jerry, said I'd only get a B. It does not matter what the bet was about. The important thing is that a creature who had no input into that bet, who was a total pawn in our game, was the prize I won. She was a coatimundi. I feel terrible now that I was a part of this.

My niece reminded me of this incident, modified by family legend. She was removed from her home somewhere in South America, removed from everything familiar, and purchased for me in a cage. I had seen her in a local store, and because I just love animals, I wanted her. This is the problem with writing about memories. At the time I wanted her, she was bought for me because I love animals. Now, because I love animals, I would never buy a wild animal being held captive in a cage. People change in the fifty-five years between now and then. What has not changed is my deep affection and admiration of animals.

A coatimundi looks like the love child of a raccoon and an anteater. They are agile climbers, have long, ringed tails, and use their front paws like hands. I named her Cinnamon because of her lovely color. She was a character. When I flew home to Virginia, I brought her with me. She was interested in every leg of the trip. When I got to my parents' home she happily walked out of her cage and to the top shelf of the tallest bookcase. She loved eggs, and if I handed her a raw egg, she would bite off the end and use her amazingly nimble tongue to lap out the egg, delivering to me the still intact eggshell. My dad once offered her a tiny dish of ice cream. Cinnamon put her hand into the bowl and, surprised at the cold, she quickly shook her paw to get that cold stuff off. Then she licked her paw to clean it. *Wait. That tasted good.* She eyed her bowl warily. *Hmm.* She put her paw in again. *Yup. Still cold.* She licked her paw right away. A whole new experience! Ice cream eaten pawful at a time. She loved it. We loved her.

My parents had an elderly cocker spaniel that they had owned for about twelve years. The dog was not a let's-just-all-get-along kind of animal. He never had been, and as he got older, stiffer in his joints and his vision failing, he got even grumpier. Cinnamon showed no concern. She went from the top of one bookcase to another, occasionally using my mom's drapes as highways.

One day, Cinnamon was quietly sleeping in her favorite perch on the tallest bookshelf. The dog was asleep at the base of the bookcase. On the top shelf was a clock that chimed ship's hours. When the clock bonged the first time, Cinnamon woke with a gigantic startle and ran down the bookcase with such speed that she literally knocked the dog over in her headlong flight. Up the closest drapes she ran. All the while keeping her eyes NOT on the aged dog, but on that noisy clock. Of course, the clock did not do anything else, so Cinnamon slowly regained her favorite perch despite the bonging clock. The cocker spaniel was possibly embarrassed. I have no idea. But he just decided to ignore her after that.

Ultimately Cinnamon went to live at an animal rescue facility. They did not have another coati for her to play with, but they offered her a big enclosure with trees. If I had it in my power, I would have returned her to the wild. Or perhaps she was bred in captivity. I don't know, and that I do not know is just awful. She was a living entity; she was a whole universe. She was wonderful, funny, mischievous, and so she was removed from everything she knew. I hate that I was a part of that.

Clara

I want to tell you a story. I have written about his incident before, but it continues to haunt me. I finally figured out why. I blamed the wrong person.

I was convinced to take a class in Victorian Poetry by a friend who was a few years older. The professor was deeply loved, a hold-over from the time FSU was FSCW. This would be his swan song. He was retiring. I could not miss the opportunity to be in his class. He was elderly, white hair, bow tie, crisp white shirt each day. He told us that a certain dogwood was in full bloom, and the entire class would make sure they went to see it. Venus was in conjunction with Mars, and the whole class would be on Landis Green, star-gazing. The "whole class" included Clara, one of two first black students admitted to FSU. We sloped through the Rubyiat and Rosetti. We adored his gentlemanly, sensitive ways. We were smitten.

One day, he walked in and told the class he had seen the film *Tom Jones* over the weekend. He had loved it and urged us all to see it, too. Clara, still imprisoned in segregation, said quietly, "I won't be able to see it."

And from the same mouth that quoted Elizabeth Barrett Browning and Tennyson came these words: "Well, that's your problem, isn't it?"

And that was where I always ended this tale of clay feet. But I was so wrong. It was me. Maybe you cannot teach sensitivity.

I did not say one word. Nothing. I should have stood up for Clara. I should have denounced the whole hideous system that kept us apart. A system that made her feel less than the person she was. I said not one word.

I knew it was wrong, I knew an innocent was being hurt, and I just sat there. If I live another fifty years, I will never forgive myself for being such a bumpkin. No. A coward. It has been fifty years since this happened. Fifty years. And all the Claras, and all their families are marching today for Black Lives Matter. Fifty years. I should have said something.

The Cliff

I am often blown away by the people who ask me to friend them on Facebook. They usually fall into two groups: The first is people I always assumed were friends and who were getting my short missives but were just too busy to respond. No biggie. I always check, do we already have friends in common? Yes, confirmed, let's be confirmed Facebook friends.

I also get requests from men I have never heard of. Never women. Men. And almost to a man they are widowers. This gives me pause. Apparently, there is a coterie of doctors, soldiers, all about twenty years younger than I am, all good looking, all living overseas, who were once married but lost a spouse and then beat an electronic path to my door.

Is that neon sign on my forehead that blinks sucker, sucker, sucker still operating? How in the world do they find me? I have a slight tremor in my hands, and when I delete their requests, I take extra care not to accidentally confirm some barely disguised potential danger. It is like looking over some bottomless relationship cliff and seeing deep into the heart of darkness. Staying safely right here, thank you.

I wonder at the lonely women who respond. Who put everything they have at risk. Put their very lives at risk, I suppose. Maybe it is an adventure. I suppose two can play the old deceit game. Come in pigeon. Yup. There it is, just over the edge of the cliff.

Clutter

My poor mother will be turning in her grave tomorrow. I am hosting my book club at the hobbit hole. Bathrooms are scrubbed, house is clean, and my wonderful cousin, David, sent me dates stuffed with bleu cheese mousse. The bad is that I have pulled inside not only my 70 approximate orchids, but other plants that have lived outside for many years when it just has not gotten this cold. If Kent and I working together could lift it, it is now in the house. We could film *Jungle Book* in here. Oh, and occasionally, a tiny frog emerges from one of the orchid pots thinking: *It is nice and warm! Is it spring already?* We have to get them safely outside before you-know-who discovers them.

I have to remind you that orchids not grown in green houses are not in bloom now. We are not talking about 70 BLOOMING orchids. We are talking about a lot of old orchids, not blooming, with long aerial roots reaching out of their pots. I do not know anyone who grows orchids for their leaves and sculptural design. Naked orchids can look healthy, but they are not known for their beauty. In fact, they can be a bit creepy with all those reaching roots.

The master bathroom has one of those big, jetted tubs that no one in our age group would ever try to enter or leave. It is a broken hip waiting to happen. It is filled and surrounded with pots at the moment. So, potentially a guest could be using the facilities when a small frog hurls itself from the tub to a large mirror. It happened to me yesterday. But I have come to expect wildlife sightings in our home. Book club ladies may not be quite as cavalier.

People have remarked in the past that my home in its expecting-company-mode, plants outside, nothing in the tub, planters in the entryway, no flashing glimpses of wildlife, reminds them of a museum. Okay. I do have a lot of stuff on the walls. But they ought to see it right now. Five of my really good friends are about to have the rainbows stripped from their eyes.

Color

There was some deep primordial need my younger brother and I had every Sunday that drove us to the ocean we kept in the front hall closet of our little house in Hutchinson, Kansas. First, we'd remove the few things that were stored in this closet. This left us a completely empty closet, just a few empty hangers on a steel rod and a small square of wood floor. Then, of course, we needed a package of Mallomars. We'd close the door behind us, sit cross-legged on the floor and be immediately lost at sea. It was pitch-black in there, but Larry and I described to one another the color of the green waves and foam that floated our little raft. Flying fish with rainbows of light caught in their wings sailed by, schools of yellow fantasy fish, garish octopi and every fish of every ocean lived in that closet.

The Mallomars were necessary to stand in for the rations we ate of raw fish. Generations before sushi came to America, we ate a lot of raw fish. We could feel the raft lift and fall on the waves, we felt the sun, tasted the salt. Ate another Mallomar.

I've never been comfortable with beige. Subtle color leaves me hungry for cobalt blue, sunfish yellow, screaming vermilion. It is like food prepared with only salt and pepper – no garlic, curry or cumin. It is as if a sort of sensory deprivation set in in Kansas: a craving for color that could only be satisfied by fantasy. I have read that art is a collaboration between God and the artist. In Kansas, someone wasn't holding up his end of the bargain.

Cooking with Molly

I love to cook, and until standing on my feet became a limiting problem, I could be found experimenting and even writing a couple of cookbooks or compiling them. So, cooking shows have grabbed my attention before. I want to draw your attention to Molly Yeh who is, get ready for this, half Jewish and half Chinese and lives on a sugar beet farm on the border of North Dakota and Minnesota. Her show is called *Girl Meets Farm* and is funny and delightful.

Let's start with the fact that the kitchen she cooks in is not anyone's idea of a trophy kitchen. I would say it is about the size of mine, and I have frequently described mine as one step above an EZ Bake Oven. When she opens her small fridge, the freezer section is a small glove compartment in the upper right corner. Remember those? Had to be defrosted by hand and held almost nothing. So, it is real. It does not hurt that she is a dead ringer for Jessica Alba.

Molly bakes her own challah and bagels and made some pastrami stuffed egg rolls the other day. She is fearless. Her new food on the farm is the hot dish. A casserole of course. Not something she might have had in Chicago where she grew up, or New York City where she met her husband. They were attending Julliard if I have my story straight. She also mastered a kind of Norwegian flatbread called lese that looks sort of like a crepe. It is served at celebratory times.

Her Chinese dad, her Jewish mom, her sisters and in-laws all come to visit. Everyone cooks. Butter has an important role in many, many recipes. Molly puts sprinkles on almost every possible dessert. She and husband, Nick, keep their Christmas tree permanently "decorated" and just bring the tree up from the basement whenever they want to. She celebrates Chanukah, he celebrates Christmas. They both celebrate one another. They are great fun. Unpretentious, very hard-working, very young.

When the camera pulls away at the end of the show, her home is all alone and surrounded by fields as far as the eye can see. And snow. One would have to be resourceful.

Find her on the Food Network.

Covid Chronicles 5: 4/13/20

March 13, 2020 was the last time I went to a restaurant. I went to celebrate a friend's birthday. The whole book club was invited, but we were already being warned not to gather in groups. But it was Nonnie's birthday, and I could not bring myself to cancel it.

When my husband and I retired about eight years ago we downsized and reinvented ourselves. We have been very happy in retirement. It is all swept away now because we like being with other people. The single most forbidden act during a pandemic, gathering with friends, is what we most like to do. We are gregarious by nature. Hopefully some of this will come back as the danger passes. As of April 13, 2020, this is what we miss.

1. Number one on my list is water aerobics. I was a six-day-a-week regular in the 7AM class. The others in the class had become good friends. We worked out, laughed, talked about our families, shared recipes. We celebrated one another's birthdays, and we laughed. A lot. Rain or shine, we showed up. It was a mark of commitment for us. We now Zoom at 7 each Friday morning. It is so wonderful to see those faces and hear their voices. But, of course, it is a mere shadow of what we had.

2. OLLI classes. We were about half-way through the semester when the bottom fell out of our society. I

was taking the most wonderful classes: The American Musical from Oklahoma through Hamilton; Pathway to War; Ancient Greece in the Modern Mind. Each one was outstanding. And though they were finished online in what the schools euphemistically call "distance learning", it just did not compare to the wonderful interaction we had with our professors and fellow students when we were in a classroom. In contradiction to our local paper announcing we were thriving, in fact, we are scraping by. This is not the OLLI I have come to know and love.

3. Book club. Let me be honest. I belong to three book clubs but only regularly attend one. The reason has nothing to do with the quality of the gatherings. Each is amazing in its own way. But I do not like to drive at night anymore. So, now I attend through Zoom one of the book clubs that I was not regularly attending. I am told at least one of the others will also go to Zoom. My prediction is a lot more talk about the books and a lot less wine.

4. Sunday with Marty and Beth. My brother and sister-in-law moved here about five years ago, and we have been getting together once a week ever since. We alternate between our homes, and besides a good meal, we watch a movie, a series, something. We talk. We are family. We do holidays and birthdays together. Last summer, Marty was diagnosed with cancer. I am grateful for every minute that we have together, and a pandemic that keeps us isolated is using up our valuable time. Tick tock. None of us is immortal.

5. Movies, concerts, plays, symphonies, art shows, art in the park, brunch at Kool Beanz or The Egg;

dinner anywhere with friends, lunch with my girlfriends, shopping in Thomasville.

6. Haircuts and pedis! I look more like Howard Hughes every day.

7. Grocery shopping. I love grocery shopping. I always go to the same store, greet the employees, take my time seeing what is new [Have you tried Sumo citrus? To die for.] and try mightily to remember to bring my own bags into the store with me. They are in the car. I see neighbors and friends. I feel like part of a community. My groceries are now delivered. Not the same at all.

8. Shopping at Tallahassee Nurseries. Yes, they have been enormously kind and delivered right to my doorstep. But the joy and sheer exhilaration of walking through those grounds and greenhouses is lost. My mom and I told Gene Ellis years [and years] ago that he should charge an entrance fee. Luckily, he kindly laughed and ignored me. How can I know what plants I cannot live without until I have spent an hour or more carefully considering the finely curated beauty on display.

9. My grandchildren. Listen, if you marry well in old age, you get a fabulous package deal: one spouse, a child or two, and grandchildren! And man did I marry well. Of course, my husband is standard setting, and his children, civil and inclusive. But those little boys just have my heart and I have no intention of taking it back. What a deal! They live in Central Florida, and again, we visit online almost daily. Not the same, not the same, not the same. You cannot get that little boy smell online.

10. Sports. I am not even remotely a sports fan, but the people I love are sports fans. BIG sports fans. I am a fan of sports fans. March Madness, cancelled. Baseball games? Cancelled. The summer Olympics? Nope. My sports intoxicated family is suffering. I came into the living room the other afternoon and found my baseball-loving husband watching a ten-year-old baseball game. Heartbreaking.

11. Travel. Having traveled throughout my life, I no longer travel. But my husband LOVES to travel, and he had a year of wonderful excursions planned. Cancelled. I love to see the people I love happy. And they are not.

Of course, I know that this is entirely frivolous. We have not lost our jobs; no one is ill; we have a home and sufficient food. We have not lost anyone we love. And in the grand scheme of things, not being able to go swimming is the loss of a privilege many never had. I know. I do have some perspective.

But it also takes a long time to invent and reinvent yourself. A lot of that has been swept away, almost overnight. I am grateful for all we had. I miss it enormously; we had won life's prize. But just coming out of this pandemic alive will be the real prize.

Creation

My parents added a garden room with a hot tub to their home. Although the associative thoughts of hot tubs run to nubile young women, white wine and sexual freedom, their granddaughter – my nine-year-old niece, Rachael – saw it for what it was: An intergalactic starship, cruising through planets and stars in the warm, gentle swirl of the watery universe.

A sudden punch of the bubbler sent her into warp drive, dodging asteroids, avoiding aliens, racing to the far curve of space. Careful manipulation of her controls and valves took Rachael to planets and cultures created within the god's eye of youth. She fought valiantly, suffered terrible wounds, endured unfathomable hardships, lost companions, made new friends with strange and wondrous abilities.

She invented mountain ranges, seas and atmospheres, where two suns lit the day and six moons rolled back the darkness of the night. Hours would pass as her skin raisined and her mind wrinkled, wrapped around problems, thought her way out of them, assumed control of her life, her universe.

She would arrive finally in her grandmother's kitchen, wrapped in a towel, her hair streaming water.

Her grandmother would ask, "What have you been doing, Rachael?"

Came the inevitable, adult-proof, bedrock reply of childhood, "Nothing."

Is this what God told his mother after he'd created the heavens and the earth?

Dad's 98th Memorial

My dad, who died in June of 2008, would have been 98 today. Although he was not a perfect person, I loved him, still love him, with something like hero worship that can neither be dimmed nor reduced by the very rare times he did not measure up to the man he wanted to be. I still weigh the rightness of things by what he would have thought. His imagined opinion.

His parents immigrated from Lithuania, then part of Mother Russia, at the time of the revolution. They escaped through Russia's frozen eastern door with four children and made their way through China, Japan, Canada to the United States. They were observant Jews. Dad was the first of the children born in this country. The Amerikaners, their sibs called them.

My grandfather wanted my dad to be a doctor. Dad wanted to fly blimps. And nothing as paltry as his culture and the expectations of his family was going to hold him back. Nothing as paltry as being a Jew and the son of immigrants was going to hold him back, mold him. He had other ideas and saw himself as unconstrained by anything but his own abilities. He was an individual.

He contacted his senator, took the test and was admitted into the United States Naval Academy at Annapolis. A famously WASPy place with its own ingrained culture of rigor, discipline, and competition, my dad thrived and loved very moment. The Navy recognized intelligence when they saw it and, as Dad complained, tried to make an "egghead" out of him.

He earned two Masters degrees. He wanted to fly blimps. And so, he did. He wanted adventure. It may be the consummate "only in America" story. He loved the country that had taken his family in, given them a place to live and work. He would be devastated by the recent insurrection, the lies, the democratic failures. He believed fiercely in our democratic processes.

Happy Birthday, Papasan. Marty and I keep you in our hearts and in our memories.

Dancing With Harry

Sometimes, when I dream, I'm dancing with Harry. I always thought we were just the right size for one another. He is just an inch to two taller than I am, so we could talk or laugh or sing to one another while we danced. I always felt sorry for those miniature women clutched to the belt buckle of an overhanging lurch of a man. Equally to be pitied are the women whose mates seemed just tall enough to pillow their heads on their breasts, all the while madly pumping their arms up and down, hoping to prime those dry wells.

Neither of us is a trained dancer or anything, but our enthusiasm carried us along nicely. Once, while we were visiting in Tokyo, some Japanese friends invited us to their tango club. There, in the formal ballroom of an exquisite Japanese hotel, hundreds of Japanese were moving through the stylized patterns of the tango. We watched for a while as partners glided by, their heads, hips and hands carving the Japanese air into Argentine intricacies.

"We can do this," Harry said. "Come on."

Cheek to cheek, our arms thrust out before us, we stepped and turned, posed and whipped our heads. We were having a grand time, laughing and feeling the insidious heat of the music, when we realized that the other dancers had cleared the floor and were circled round, applauding us. What a coup! What a couple of fakes we were!

There were years when we and five other couples ate and danced at one another's homes monthly. We called ourselves a "Gourmet Group," but hyperbole was always in the air with these expansive people. Of course, I did have to share him. I have no idea how it started, but Harry and Walter Tschinkel always wound up having one dance together.

Sometimes at home, while cleaning the kitchen and listening to the radio, some song we loved would come on, and we'd stop whatever we were doing and dance across the linoleum, the dogs watching us in wonder. Jitterbug or foxtrot, fast or slow, some songs simply cannot be resisted.

I have pictures of us dancing at family weddings and bar mitzvahs over the years. Sometimes, our eyes are closed. Most of the time we're laughing.

When Harry was still in the rehab hospital after his stroke, I entered his room one morning to find him standing in the middle of the floor. He limped over, put his left arm around my waist and took my right hand in his. As we swayed gently back and forth, I sang him one of our favorite songs. I like to think he was telling me that we're going to keep on moving through life together.

The Day After

The presidential election is too close to call this morning, but whoever wins, I am once again struck with how totally out of touch I am with the people who surround me. I thought for sure that Trump's lies and incompetent handling of nearly every facet of his time in office would slam him up against a big, blue wall this season. No. What people care about in this country is not other people. What they care about is their 401k's, their investments, the stock market. They care about money. You can do anything to anyone, commit sins of commission and omission so long as the money is doing well. How can I keep forgetting this? We are capitalists. Money is all. And as my mother-in-law used to say, rich or poor, it never hurts to have money. It almost doesn't matter who wins because this is who we are. We are revealed.

I truly, naively, thought better of us. I am such a true believer. There was no cheating, no fraud. Just everyday people going to the polls and voting. And there are so very many who are not like me at all. It is me who does not get it. It is me swimming upstream once again.

I was encouraged by many local elections turning out the way I thought they should. Here in my tiny blue bubble. I send congratulations to Rocky Hanna, Loranne Ausley, Allison Tant. Please carry on my deep blue baton. I'm going to take a breather. I'm exhausted.

Dear President Biden

Dear President Biden,

I have never written a President before, but I had a deep hunger to write your name: President Biden. I wanted to be first in line. What a roller coaster this week has been. As self-appointed diva of doom, I was in full voice on Tuesday and am now optimistic enough to write this note. You must have tremendous inner resources to have gone through this terrible week and know all you will have to muster to get through the next eleven weeks, and then the next four years. But I am in full Pollyanna mode and utterly convinced that once you have slain the ogre of Pennsylvania Avenue, all wishes will be granted. So, I have a list:

1. Please choose the very best people you can for every single appointment. Please put someone who loves our parks and nature in charge of them. Please give us back our post office and banish Mr. DeJoy to some nether region. Promise that you will never, under any circumstances, put someone in charge of a department that he or she has attempted to destroy. There are some remarkable people in this country. Find them and ask them to serve this country by sharing their love with all of us. Restore the Clean Water Act. Protect Alaska's wilderness, and ban timbering there.

2. Join the fight against Climate Change. Seek out our best scientists, and ask them to guide us on how we can stop climate change, and how to protect ourselves from foreseeable dangers. What can we do to help the west with its fires and the gulf and east coast from ferocious hurricanes? Show us a path, let us have a national plan.

3. Speaking of plans, please ask Dr. Fauci to create his dream team of doctors, researchers, planners to bring Covid-19 to heel. Have a national plan to diminish its effects and a plan to distribute vaccine to everyone. Please speak truthfully and openly to us of how long we will need to self-isolate. [I miss my grandsons.] If you could do this at least once a week, discuss how the battle is going, it would be helpful. I know that we have learned an immense amount about this disease since last February. More people who are hospitalized are living through the disease. What else do we know now? Make mask wearing mandatory unless you are in your own home.

4. Pay off the student loans of all doctors, nurses, physicians' assistants, med tech, or other health care workers.

5. Stacy Abrams registered somewhere between 800,000 and 1,000,000 people to vote in Georgia. She is smart and resourceful. Our country needs her. Pete Buttigieg, Bernie Sanders, Elizabeth Warren, Amy Klobuchar have a love for this country that is palpable. Find places in your cabinet for their hard work and dedication to the good things America has stood for.

6. Never give another cent to religious schools or private schools of any ilk. Restore public education to children of all ages and abilities. Pay off every teacher's student loans.

7. Tax the rich.

8. Expand the Affordable Care Act.

9. Let it be known that violence against people of color by the police will be aggressively prosecuted.

10. When people die, when there are natural disasters that cost your citizens everything they have worked for in their lives, when children are hurt or lost, please show that you feel the pain their families feel. Please show that their grief is heard.

11. Please make it unambiguously clear that you oppose vigilantism, white supremacy, the Ku Klux Klan, The Proud Boys, racism, antisemitism, bigotry and hate in all its many forms and faces. Give them no air time.

12. Please speak out for the wonderful achievements of Americans who win the Nobel Prize, are named Poet Laureate, who bring honor and awe to our nation. Praise the writers, the artists, the filmmakers, the chemists, the biologists, the clever engineers and inventors. Give us pride in our people. Give them air time.

13. Restore our professional state department and return Caroline Kennedy as ambassador to Japan. Restore Col. Vinland and the other truth tellers to their posts with the thanks of a grateful nation.

14. Take down the walls around the White House, the fences, the barriers. Build roads, bridges.

15. Never again separate families from one another. Reunite the children we still have in detention with their parents. It is our most solemn duty. Do not build detention camps. Period. Defund and dissolve ICE. Develop a humane and compassionate immigration policy that we can point to with pride.

16. This is a hard one. You are not a kid anymore. I wish you the best of health and longevity, but I ask you to plan for the worst. Please talk to your capable Vice President about what if. Make her a part of all you do.

And mostly, Mr. President, more than any other thing I am going to wish for, never lie to us. And do not lie to yourself. Not big lies, not little lies because you think we will worry. Tell us the complete and absolute truth. Restore our trust.

Make us proud to be Americans again.

Wishing you and all of us four years of renaissance,

Paula Walborsky

Dearest Ring

Thirty-two years ago, when Harry Walborsky changed my marital status and last name, we went to a local jewelry store to buy a ring to symbolize our marriage. A lover of Victorian poetry and prose, I explained that a "dearest" ring would really mean the most to me. Here's how it works: The ring is set with stones, and the first letter of each stone spells out the message. So, "dearest" would be diamond, emerald, amethyst, ruby, emerald, sapphire, topaz. The stones, of course, circle the band, so you have to know where to start in order to decipher the message. Frequently the Victorians spelled out "regards" (ruby, emerald, garnet, amethyst, ruby, diamond, sapphire). I thought "regards" just a tad distant for a wedding ring, however.

The jeweler had no Victorian rings but showed us a band with seven assorted stones. We added it up and realized that seven was the right number of spaces for "dearest", and so we bought it with the idea that on each of our first seven anniversaries, we would have one stone changed until it read "dearest." Romance is my middle name, and I loved the idea of the "dearest" taking shape as our married life progressed.

On our first anniversary, we appeared before the same jeweler, handed him my band and said, like a small cheerleading squad, "Give us a D!"

"Oh," he said coolly, "the stones in this band can't be changed."

We protested. He demurred. We went home with my band reading "gazorten" or "tengazor" or "zortenga", depending on where you started.

What the heck, I figured. I knew the secret message, and spelling Walborsky was achievement enough.

The Death of Hope

Ruth Bader Ginsberg died yesterday. She was a small, slight woman in stature. Quite lovely as a young woman. And somewhere within that small frame was the strongest fiber ever known. She lived her life as a Jewish woman in a world that values neither women nor Jews.

She became a trailblazing lawyer, seeking and winning, gender equality cases. She was appointed to the United States Supreme Court, the second woman to serve. And although she steadfastly continued her quest for justice and equality, she was also best friends with Antonin Scalia the most conservative voice to sit on the court, some might argue. They were philosophical opposites. Yet their mutual respect, trust, and friendship burgeoned in spite of her dissents, his reading of the Constitution in its most limiting way. They had fun together. Their mutual love of opera was the basis for costumes and laughter. They believed in one another's goodness, irrespective of how blinkered they thought an opinion might be.

The Supreme Court is a cloistered place. The justices and their clerks [the brightest minds from their law schools] go through daily rituals that tell them where they sit on the bench, who assigns cases, who writes for the majority, and how opinions are circulated. Appointed for life, some, like Ginsburg, stay for the duration of their lives. Others retire. They are supposed to be removed from the pressures of politics by this tenure. That tenure is supposed to last and be ever more informed as Congresses and Presidents come and go. They are the conscience of the country. They are nine people who, when they want to, can shake the world. And they can make mistakes. They are, after all, human.

During my seventy-five years, they have done away with separate but equal, but also decided that corporations are people. Every single justice has a huge impact, whether it be from an assertion of personality and the ability to sway his/her peers, or from consistently being the Me Too voice to a dominant justice, lending weight to his/her vote.

Her loss belies her tiny stature. Her death is a loss to her family and to us first because she is a feminist icon. She considered herself a "flaming feminist". She is a hero, a giant to young women all over this country. She is deeply loved and respected. But her loss also means that her place on the bench is vacant. There is a void. And nature and politics hate a void.

Her death comes at a time when our country is perilously close to civil war. The President has appointed people to run the many agencies and bureaus who in fact want to dismantle the very agencies they are appointed to lead. These appointees are always just "acting directors", so no appointments have to be approved by Congress. Even the post office is being vandalized. His lower court appointments are inexperienced and clearly chosen for their political leanings. A brick-by-brick dismantling of the American government is underway. To this Trumpian reality comes this vacancy. It is a huge, gaping wound. The loss of an icon that can now be filled with whatever judicial detritus Trump wants to use to undermine the sanctity, the elevation of the highest court in the land. It is an entire wall of bricks torn away from our governing strength.

Justice Ginsberg knew all of this and much more. She wanted so badly to live past the election in hopes that a new President would appoint her replacement, well, successor. No one will replace her. Her dying wish was that the President permit the election two months from now to decide who that person will be. It would be simple, fundamental fairness if one President was treated like his successor.

Fundamental fairness. It was a feather weight of hope. She must have known that there was no possibility that this President cared a fig about her dying wish. And for my beloved country, her death is the death of hope that equality and diversity, jurisprudence, will continue to find protections at the Supreme Court's bench.

The Denim Bridge

Yesterday, I finally did it. It needed to be done for weeks. Okay, maybe months.

My favorite pair of jeans crossed the denim bridge yesterday. I realize that "distressed", holey, scuffed, and frayed jeans are now considered in their prime. But mine were, I can now admit, way past stressed. They were moribund.

The waist band was detaching, and it is hard not to see that as a cruel and accurate metaphor for my covid life. They were my best friends. Always comfy and soft, washed almost daily for years, they accepted my body without comment. They had watched all of *Game of Thrones* and all *The Good Wife*. They sat through dozens and dozens of novels and biographies over the years. They had gone to Tallahassee Nurseries, and they had cooked latkes and other things that can be expected to spatter grease. They never flinched.

They matched anything I wanted to wear, anywhere I wanted to go. They were a light blue and are often disparagingly called "grandma jeans" because they had an elastic waist and were generous through the seat and thighs. In other words, they matched me perfectly. Two pockets that endearingly refused to dry short of three times through the drier. Long enough, but not fall down too long. They were as perfect as jeans come.

When I bought them, I bought two identical pairs. There is no such thing, of course. I could tell her from her twin sister immediately. She just had a certain je ne sais quoi. She was the poet of words, the composer of music, the artist of paints and Olympic athlete of jeans. Gone now. I will grieve her for a very long time. Her sister and I are getting used to one another. Her grip is a bit too tight. Huh.

Distracted

I belong to a small book club that gathers once a month on a Friday afternoon. We are old, abstemious, and read anything we want to. There is no "chosen" book. Somehow, many of this coterie are mystery lovers. Over the years, we have had times when one of us says, "I haven't read a thing. I cannot concentrate on the words, cannot take in the plot, the characters." This last week, there were two of us, and although the others had read, their intake/output had fallen sharply. So, what could be distracting some of the brightest people I know? That is our collective mystery.

Is it the pandemic that is giving us a sixth wave that everyone seems to be ignoring? Is that the distractor? Over one million dead and counting in our country alone. Is it the scandal at the Supreme Court where Justice Thomas and his wife have shockingly disgraced the court's ethics? Or is it the leaked unfinished draft of how Roe v. Wade will be overturned by precedents set by an English judge who officiated at witch trials? Women will die again. There is a war in Ukraine, and the peoples of Africa are already feeling the effects of famine. Ukrainians are dying, Russians are dying. It is a war. And one side has nuclear weapons.

Perhaps the problem is the random killing. Child-slaughter is a term I heard on NPR. But it can be anyone who is a "soft target". That means, unarmed, unsuspecting, easy to kill. In grocery stores, schools, concerts, churches and synagogues random people, unarmed, giving offense to no one are slaughtered. Guns are everywhere, 65 million more guns in this country than every man, woman, and child. Apparently, figuring out how to regulate this is beyond the abilities of those who somehow manage to tax us. They can get to our money, freeze our assets, but they just cannot figure out how to handle the gun problem.

We have a proud military history in my family, and although I never thought we lived up to promises like equality before the law, equality in all things, I felt we were making progress. Women and minorities had never had more freedom in any other time and place in our history. Inch by litigious inch, we had moved forward.

My friends who are gay or trans ask how life will be when their very existence is illegal.

It is the beginning of another hurricane season. But really, that is just weather. The wars, the famines, the murders are all committed by one man. A white man. Acting alone. Raining hell on us.

Distracted? No. Heartbroken. We are grieving for our lost chance at Camelot.

Dr. Fauci Day

I saw online somewhere that December 24th was Dr. Fauci's 80th birthday, and Washington, D.C. through him a birthday party. What a great idea.

Expanding on this idea, I want a Dr. Fauci Day every year. It can be his birthday, or perhaps on his half birthdays to spread the fun out. He may not want an airport named for him, but how about the most amazing, international, cutting-edge research facility? Something researchers would drool over and keep us protected and well for generations to come.

There should be a reading of the Hippocratic Oath at high noon, and all health care providers will be treated to ten days of uninterrupted vacation. People will don funny masks and dance in the streets as close to one another as they can be, sanitizer will be left in the bathrooms of all across the nation. Researchers will relate stories of how other vaccines and other researchers saved us from small pox, polio, measles, diphtheria. Our children will be awestruck.

Heroes! We have heroes among us every day. And everyone will eat Italian food because everyone loves Italian food. Our first borns will all be named for him, and there will be thousands and thousands of baby Tonys and Tonis. We will send thank you cards to his entire family, and movies will be made about how he slew the pandemic dragon in spite of the obstacles thrown in his way. How he spoke truth to power. How he not only survived but saved us from ourselves.

Anthony Fauci's name should become synonymous with selfless devotion to the truth, and to mankind. We need a grassroots movement here. Anthony Fauci Day!

Covid Chronicles 6: 4/27/20

We are now six weeks into quarantine. Depending on whom you believe, we may be half-way through, finished, or have a very long way to go. We are being very cautious and are not relaxing our vigilance. We are in and staying in.

Our groceries are being delivered to us. It has caused me to reflect on the magic of a grocery store. There are several well-known chains within a couple of miles of us, but I am a big fan of Publix. I have found their customer service to be exceptional. They earned my loyalty. Not that I don't enjoy an occasional dalliance with Fresh Market or Trader Joe's, but they are just one-night stands.

My heart belongs to Publix. Berries out of season, fruits, and vegetables from all over the world. If you want fresh asparagus in the spring, they have them. If you want fresh asparagus in December, they have them. They have a wide variety of meats for the carnivores among us. In addition to the usual chicken, goose, duck, beef, pork, lamb they have ostrich on occasion. And now, they have that meat that is plant based. And buffalo. But I'm not really doing the meat department justice.

Let's take chicken. A staple in any non-veg person's plan. They have whole chicken, skin and bones in their proper places. They have boneless and skinless breasts and thighs. And thighs and breasts with skin and bones intact. They have chicken cutlets and chicken quarters. They have chicken wings, chicken livers, chicken gizzards and hearts. Chicken tenderloins. Chicken tenders. They have frozen chickens and not frozen chicken. Roasting chicken, stewing chicken and frying chickens.

So, when my shopper/ delivery person indicated that Publix had no chicken of any kind whatsoever the other day, it rocked my world. Where had the breakdown happened? A sick stocker? Truck drivers? Illness at the poultry processing plant? Death at the poultry farm? One of the most popular grocery chains in the South has no chicken, one of the most popular meats. Especially in the South. Out of Buffalo? Sure. It can happen. But no chicken of any kind?

And the truth of all those sayings that mean you don't know what you've got till it's gone comes home to roost. In the place the chickens should be. Other things are no longer on the shelves, too. Tuna fish is rationed, the kinds in the can that are necessary for that comfort staple casserole our mothers made. Two small cans at a time. Our favorite bread is often missing.

There is nothing like an American grocery store anywhere else in the world. It is almost an icon of our multi-cultural, multi-regional nation. The amount of administration and management it takes to run each of these stores is nothing short of amazing.

Lots of perishables being shipped from all over the world. How long to keep them on the shelves? What special holidays are coming up that need special grocery stocks? At Passover, when lots of us old Jewish bubbys are making chopped liver, Publix has fresh chicken liver for sale. And briskets. Candies just for Easter. Chocolate rabbits with their tempting ears. Halloween candy, candy canes. And what is the demography of those living close enough to any individual store? Tough job.

The people showing up for work each day at grocery stores are putting themselves in harm's way. They do it because we have to eat. They have to eat. If ever there was an essential business, it is grocery stores.

I am so grateful that you are there to keep this essential part of our civilization working. I am more than grateful, but for once, words fail me. The empty cases where chicken was once for sale, tell me in a very real way how profound this epidemic is. When you are back to your top form, I will know we have come through to the other side.

Dragons Love Tacos

My youngest grandchild, Beckett the Beautiful, loves the book *Dragons Love Tacos*. In the way of children everywhere, reading it through one time just whets his whistle for reading it again. And again. And again.

If Ted Cruz [you bet I know who you are] is right, I should be either a dragon or a taco very soon now. And my brother, Larry, should have morphed into a choo-choo train because we read *The Little Engine That Could* to him so many times that it literally fell apart. Well, it did fall into the bathtub accidentally once.

My sister-in-law, Beth, is a voracious reader of mysteries. It is not an exaggeration at all to say that she has read hundreds of them. If a murder is committed in her neighborhood, I'm lookin' straight at Beth. And she will get away with it!

How about all those thousands upon thousands of people who love spy stories? OMG. Breeding right there in our bookstores and flying into our homes through Amazon and Kindle. Can the FBI even hope to keep an eye on all of them? You know, a lot of people read the *Communist Manifesto*, and Mao's *Little Red Book*, Hitler's *Mein Kampf*. Decades after they were written, these books are still read!

A library is just a big stove with pots bubbling away with all kinds of possible insurrection, revolution, change of order, change of regime, looking for someone to fill with thoughts.

Plans. You can learn how armies are organized, how battles are fought, how to build bombs. Big bombs.

Of course, there are also books on how to defuse bombs. Books on how civilizations are built are available. The works of scientists, philosophers, people who revolutionized the very way we think about life are also available.

Once this cauldron of dangers comes to the attention of Cruz and his followers, I assume libraries are going to be abolished. Apparently, they have flown under his personal radar so far, but surely, one day, he will accidentally stumble into that hotbed of neurological fitness. Brains being exercised. The potentiality is frightening.

Edgar Booth

The first lawyer I worked with after law school was Edgar Booth. He hired me and then forgot to tell his partners about it. When I reported for work to a previously all male firm, it was not a happy day.

I, of course, knew nothing about this. I assumed they were aware of my existence and were waiting for me to appear. When I did report for work, Edgar called me into his huge office where I perched nervously on the edge of my seat while he talked to me about the financial side of practicing law. I did not hear a word. I was so nervous that the blood was pounding in my ears, and I could not hear anything.

He looked at me a bit strangely sometimes, and I think I nodded when I should have shaken my head. He said the other lawyers would not be happy I was there because I would be taking cases from them. *Um, whaaat?* Then he said I did not have an office and showed me to the library.

I sat down and looked at the books. When it was time to go home, I walked into my house and burst into tears. It was not a propitious beginning. But Edgar Booth made me into a lawyer, and I owe him many thanks.

One of the secretaries was moved from her office, and I was given that office. I was assigned a brief to write. Edgar walked in and asked how the brief was going. I showed him my first draft to read and explained I was on my second draft. I had taught legal writing and research at the law school. I felt like I knew what I was doing. This was before we had memory typewriters or word processing programs. I wrote in long hand on legal tablets, literally cutting paragraphs with scissors and pasting with scotch tape.

"Stop," he said. He took away my tablet with my draft on it. "This is a Dictaphone. You speak your brief in here, and a secretary types it on the other end. You dictate a brief. This draft and redraft takes too long. Holy moly." And he walked out of the office with my tablet in his hand.

My desk was covered with case books, opened statutes, my notes. I sat there and thought about it for a while. *How to do this?* Like eating an elephant, as the proverb goes. One bite at a time.

I made an outline. I found the cases I needed and arranged them according to the outline. And I started over with my summary of argument. I am not sure it saved any time to dictate the first brief. I had to remember to tell the typist at the other end, open paren, capital letter, comma, all the information of how it should look on a page. Capital letters, lower case, punctuation, block indent quote, footnotes! There was a lot to keep in your mind simultaneously.

I imagined Becky, secretary extraordinaire, sitting there as I spoke to her. It helped. But slowly, I realized not only could I do this, but it was wonderful for when I was in court. You have to gather all the facts and all the law together into a cogent whole to explain it to a judge or jury. You cannot read to people. It puts them to sleep. If you dictated whole briefs, argument in court just fell into place. It was a bit like being dropped off the end of the legal dock and being told to swim. But guess what? I did it!

I do not think Edgar ever changed a word in any of my briefs. It does not matter. My briefs often won, and in one case, a judge on the District Court of Appeal complimented me from the bench on my well-written brief. I thought I had died and gone to heaven. Thank you, Edgar. Thank you a thousand times over for teaching me the skill of organizing my thinking so I could argue in court, argue wherever I needed to. Hard thing to teach. Great teacher.

Eighteenth Anniversary of Harry's Death

We would have been married fifty years this November, but he died eighteen years ago after only thirty-two years of marriage. He was an enormous influence in my life. None of it should have worked, of course. He was twenty-two years older than I was, had four children who despised me (from an earlier marriage) and a brother who did everything he could to undermine our connection to one another.

The family sent Harry a letter saying that they would not have anything to do with him until and unless he divorced me. He never showed me the letter. I found it long after his death in files being cleared out for a move. So many things made sense after I found that letter. Harry was diagnosed with cancer in the 80s, and he made it clear I was not to tell anyone in his family. Hard stop. No one. I wrote some oblique letters, hoping one or more would call. They did not. Harry said, "Cancer is not something you base a relationship on."

It is hard to say why our relationship worked so well. But it did. I adored him, loved him with every fiber of my being. I called him Hesh or Heshele. I thought he was drop-dead gorgeous and so smart. And although I sometimes wonder now at the remove of the eighteen years since his death, at the time I was completely convinced it was a totally reciprocated love.

We went through so much together. We clung to one another. He supported me, encouraged me, was my biggest fan. He told me I was brilliant and beautiful. He loved my cooking, loved the way his friends took to me with ease. We talked nonstop, never one of those couples who sit in a restaurant silently looking around with nothing to say to one another. We told our life stories to one another, talked politics, talked about everything. There were no limits, no secrets. Well, I did not have any secrets.

Then Harry collapsed while giving a lecture, perhaps in Germany or France. It was decided when he returned that he needed a carotid endarterectomy. I was terrified. I knew with a frightening certainty that he was going to die, and a good friend came to be with me during his surgery. The doctors assured us and reassured us that this surgery was very common and had a 98% success rate. Doctors abuse statistics regularly this way, and I was frantic with worry. But he came through the surgery just fine, and I saw him in the recovery room smiling at me, teasing me for my needless worry.

I went home that night while Harry stayed overnight in intensive care. The call came about four in the morning. "Mrs. Walborsky, you need to get here immediately. Your husband is unresponsive." I was there five minutes later, and Harry was lying in bed with his eyes open. He could not speak or move his right side.

I held him and kissed him. A huge clot had formed at the site of the surgery and closed all arterial flow to the brain on that side. Oxygen was not reaching his brain. Later, imaging showed that fully half his brain had been damaged. They warned me that he would most likely die, and every time they checked him, they told me the same thing, he could not be expected to live with his brain so badly damaged. But live he did. For eight more years the talker, the raconteur, the lecturer, singer, gadfly, jokester was silenced by global aphasia. Certainly, the Harry Walborsky who had been was no more.

Aphasia means that your brain no longer processes language. Global means that both receptive and expressive language are broken. Harry could talk, but what he said, over and over and over again was, "One-one." One one, one one, one one, one one. If asked to read from a book, he did not hesitate: "One one, one one, one one." With emphasis, pauses.

Could he understand spoken language? Who knows. If asked to stick out his tongue, he might raise a hand. But sometimes, when he was very relaxed and not being tested, he seemed to understand things I might say. "Can I get you a cup of coffee? No, thank you." And he retained swear words I had never, ever heard him say aloud.

Then his cancer came back and went straight to his bones. And then he had a cascade of other strokes. Many years after the fact, the doctors who treated his cancer with radiation think that the radiation undermined his vascular system. And we fought the cancer and worked to rehab the damage that accumulated from the strokes. And somehow, I morphed from his wife to his mother. I had to take away his car keys. Tell him not to go on the roof to blow away the leaves. Few, very few adult men want to live with their mother. What an unmitigated hell for both of us.

Sometimes, I think I would give anything for five minutes more with him. But not the damaged Harry. I want to hear him talk again. I want to hear that distinctive Bronx voice. I want to tell him thank you for every moment we had together, the good ones and the bad ones, and know that he understands me.

I have gone on with my life as Harry and I discussed many times. I am a person who is enormously lucky in love. I am now very happily married to Kent Putnam. He is completely at ease with the idea that I still love my long deceased, late husband. Once you have been happily married, all you ever want to be is happily married.

Heshele, your memory is a blessing to me.

Election Day

It is Election Day 2020. It is like no Election Day I have ever lived through. Cities and towns have erected barriers to protect their stores and buildings. In a season of natural disasters, fires, and huge hurricanes, the hurricane of anarchy, of anger and fury, of disappointment at the ballot box will hit landfall as soon as the polls open this morning.

For two days, parades of Trump Trucks, huge flags waving, have driven up and down our main streets. Major roads in NJ have been closed. Roads to the polls. Ominous goons, armed, loud, and threatening wear their red Trump MAGA hats with their camouflage vests. One group in Texas attempted to force a busload of Biden staff headed for a rally off the road.

Our violence-fomenting President has had yet another huge fence put up around the White House. He does not intend to leave under any circumstances. My friends online have taken to their prayers for peace and a change of leadership. But they have hunkered down. Ninety-three million people have already voted. They want their votes to be counted, and they did not want to have to face a gauntlet of intimidation on election day. There has not even been an election yet. This is America? This is the country from which I smugly watched other countries thrash through changes in regime?

Yes, now I see the privilege I took for granted. Now I see the hundreds of years of people who played the governance game inside the lines. Of course, there were some scofflaws. But we went through the motions. Armed thugs and vigilantes did not take to the streets. We were able to gracefully go through a transfer of power. Was there disappointment? Anger? Disbelieving unhappiness? All one has to do is look back just four years. A man who lost the popular vote by over three million votes came riding into the presidency on the swayed back of the electoral college.

It is difficult to say how we got here. But the choice this year between candidates could not be more glaring. Even the noise level is different. Could there have been better opposition? I have no idea. Biden offers what looks like a safe harbor after sailing four years through treacherous seas. If the Democrats lose, that choice will be picked clean by the critics. Of course.

But if I could make some changes, I would disallow the carrying of any weapon from one week before early voting begins until January 21st. All persons of voting age are required to vote. There is a stiff fine for failure to vote or for carrying a weapon on your person or in your vehicle. Persons stealing or defacing election signs would be heavily fined. Whoever is running, whenever we have the next election, this incipient violence cannot be allowed to continue. God bless America. Stand beside her, and guide her, through the night with a light from above.

Enforced Sensibility

I frequently order books online. I see a book written up somewhere, and instead of getting on the waiting list at the library, I order one. All mine. Even though I have pledged many times to not buy a single new book until I have read all the books in our hobbit hole. But no. I never keep this promise to myself, and as my brother has pointed out, I have books stacked up in every room. I will die one day under an avalanche of books. It will be a happy death.

The NYT publishes cookbooks and has a new one where all the ingredients are to taste. There are no exact measurements, no cups, teaspoons, etc. for any recipe. This is exactly how I cook! I was dying to see this cookbook and immediately ordered one. Of course, Amazon had it. And I waited. Today I got a notice from Amazon that since my book had not arrived from the NYT in thirty days, they were canceling the order. My credit card would not be charged. DANG!

My sister-in-law, Beth, and I were looking forward to a book so attuned to our way of doing things. Before we downsized to live among the hobbits, I had a whole wall of cookbooks. I love reading cookbooks. No.

Then I opened an email from Crate and Barrel to find that three chairs I ordered were once again back ordered. I do not, in the strictest sense, need these chairs. I just want to replace the ones I have at a dining room table because I have had them for decades, and I am just not fond of them. I know, absurd. But I do absurd things sometimes. How often do I use the dining room table and chairs anyway? I wrap gifts on the dining room table because it is the biggest flat surface I have. One does not need new chairs for that. But I have been stuck in my hobbit hole nearly 24/7 for a year and some months, and I just want to change the scenery. Update, renovate, move things around, fluff it up a bit in here. I cannot travel, so I need to make another world right here. But apparently, it will not be with chairs from Crate and Barrel.

I look around me. Many of the things, most in fact, that made the cut ten years ago and came with us here are things I have loved and cherished for decades. I still cannot bring myself to get rid of them. But those dining room chairs are functional. Period. They were one of the few things I would actually get rid of in my quest for something new in the house. Heck, I cannot even get a cookbook to arrive.

And then I do that thing that many women my age do. I wonder who, if anyone, will want that dining room table, will want my forty-plus blue and white plates, will want the danzantes I brought back from Mexico or the blue pitcher that sat in my lap for the entire flight from Paris. I have no children. My nieces live far away. They and my nephews have their own sense of style and their own tastes. Even though they are in the acquisitive years, I am not quite ready to give them up.

I wonder if my stuff looks old ladyish to them? I see my stuff through such a loving eye, I know the back story to each piece, remember the day I got it.

Remember Ozymandius? His broken statue is found in the sand. It says, "Look on my works, ye mighty, and despair." He could have been just an ordinary housewife thinking her tables and tchotchkes would last for millennia.

ER

Yesterday was just glorious until about 3:45 in an afternoon that had been filled with reading, writing, and enjoying my flowers. Kent had to have some surgery at the dermatologist's office and assured me it was so minor that I need not accompany him. He drove himself to the dermatologist. It was taking quite a while because he sees an excellent dermatologist, and he was very busy. Not a problem.

Every week about 3PM, I place a three-way phone call to high school friends. Jude had asked that I call half an hour later because she had a meeting to attend. She still wasn't home at 3:30, so we decided to call her back in another half hour. It didn't happen.

About fifteen minutes later, I noticed a strange pain in my mouth as if my teeth were hurting. Then a ball of pain burst in the middle of my chest, radiating out the back and slowly rose up my neck to my jaw on both sides of my face and into my head. I was in agony and afraid I was having a heart attack. I was afraid I would die. Kent was at a doctor's appointment. I was still in my gown and bathrobe because I had spent the day reading and writing. "Don't panic," I told myself. "This will pass. Do not panic." But it did not pass. I felt as if I had a heavy weight on my chest but was not having trouble breathing, although I could not take a deep breath.

I tried to call Kent. His phone was off because he was at the doctor's. I felt I had no choice and called 911. A very nice woman talked to me about where I was, what was happening and stayed on the line until the ambulance came. The pain was excruciating, but I noted I could remember the correct answers to all the questions she asked. *What was happening to me?* I had to get to my locked front door to let the EMTs in. The backdoors were both standing open as I was enjoying the day. The 911 woman talked me to the front door. One step at a time. She was wonderful. I walk with a cane and just moving on the best of days can be a challenge. The pain in my chest, face, and head was fearsome.

Once I got to the door and she knew I was in the hands of the three men there, she hung up. I do not know her name. Such a professional. So cool. So supportive.

I can only remember the names of two of the men who fed me aspirin and took my vitals, ran a blood test, made every effort to make me comfortable. David and Angel. About the time I got the aspirin, the pain completely disappeared as quickly and unexpectedly as it had arrived. And the deepest ambivalence set it. I was afraid I was going to die. The good news is I did not die. The bad news is I made a scene fit for a diva and called people away from people who really need them. I understand that I needed a doctor just in case. But I remain deeply humiliated by what now looks like an overreaction.

All I could think was I needed to tell Kent where I was and that we had left the house with the doors standing open.

At the ER, Dr. Nimmons ran more tests and talked me through what happened. I was, and remain, deeply embarrassed to have caused so much trouble. He was abundantly kind as was my nurse, Scarlett. It was determined that, as far as his tests could tell, I was in excellent health. I had not had a heart attack. I have no underlying diseases or conditions except my age, 75, and osteoarthritis. I take one prescription drug for depression.

I felt the pain move again in my chest, this time coiled beneath my left breast. It was like a sleeping beast. It stirred and went back to sleep. More tests. Nothing.

My body is trying to tell me something, but even though I have come to those trained in the language of ailments, we are not communicating. It occurs to me that the doctor thought "heart" because I said "heart." I am not a doctor. I was just relaying what I am afraid of. I have no idea if my heart was involved at all. The tests on my heart suggest it sat this entire incident on the sidelines. I inadvertently sent the posse in the wrong direction.

It is another day, and except for a deep humiliation, I have no reason to think I have a heart issue. I have something else. I need a good tracker to put his ear to the ground of this old body and figure out what it is and which way it went. I have a follow up appointment with my family doctor.

Eric

Today is my son's birthday. This is all a bit confusing as I have no biological children, and Eric is sixty-five to my seventy-five. He is married to Gabby, and they are the parents of my granddaughter, Charlotte.

When I met Eric, he was fourteen, and I was twenty-four. He hated me on sight. His father and I were planning to marry, and to say Eric did not approve is not to put too fine a point on things. His dad and I were married for thirty-two years before his death in 2002. I think it can be said that Eric's consistency in not approving of our marriage never faltered.

Then when Charlotte was about nine or ten, Eric called and asked if I would like to read to Charlotte. Thus began a time in my life I could not foresee. I have forgotten how many books Charlotte and I read together, but I think it was more than twenty. She would read a page, and I would read a page. And Eric, Gabby, and Charlotte began to make a stop at our home as they traveled to visit his brother for Passover.

For the last several years then, I have had a relationship with Eric and his family, initiated by Eric. I asked him why once. He said, "A person cannot be loved by too many people." It is my own line.

Today, Eric is sixty-five years old. I wish him the happiest of birthdays. He is a remarkable father, and I know that sharing Charlotte with me is one of the greatest gifts he could have ever conjured. Happy Birthday, Eric. Happy, happy, happy birthday.

Every Day is Prologue

I never set out to write a book. But I write a lot for myself. It is a kind of therapy, or just plain old navel-gazing. My entire adult life, I have written short stories, what they now call flash fiction, essays, memories, whatever comes out of the end of my pen. Yes, many, many of these were written before everyone had a computer with some kind of word processing device that makes editing and composing so much easier. Long hand in a truly illegible script had to make do before that. My beloved secretary typed up many of them for me. [Why, oh why, did I think a second year of Russian in high school was a better choice than typing?] Some of the oldest of them were read on our local NPR station. Sadly, local commentators are no longer a piece of their programming.

Everything I write is as true as I can make it. Unless it is fanciful. Then it may or may not be true. This not history. It is just me putting words on paper. I really, really am flattered, deeply, that friends have asked me to compile these blurbs into a book. And more than that, my family and friends are that artesian well that fills my life to overflowing so my story floods these pages.

That is all good and well, but you need a kind of dramatis personae to help you through this. I do not always say, for example, that I was the oldest sibling and my next older brother was named Larry. We were two years and two weeks apart in age. He died many years ago when he was in his early fifties. Our baby brother, eight years younger, is named Marty.

I have no biological children. Larry had two sons; Marty had two daughters. Larry's sons are Aaron and Matthew and they have children of their own. Larry has four grandchildren.

Marty's daughters, Allison and Rachael, have given him four grandchildren, too. Our family is a balanced equation. So far. My parents are here, my grandparents, my husbands, my husbands' children and my husbands' children's spouses, my husbands' grandchildren, our friends, our pets. My extraordinary cousins. You will figure it out.

I dedicate this book to those wonderful people and to Josephine and Royal Yu, Rose and Doug Cook, John and Meg Paschal, Dick and Priscilla Dreibelbis, Jane and Reggie Butler, Helen and Larry Callaway, Judith Claremon and Roger Goldstein, to my bridge buddies Margaret Lynn Duggar, Jeanne Patterson, and Shirlee Bowne. I dedicate this to my soggy friends at water aerobics, to the instructors, to the ever-enduring life guards.

Most of all I dedicate this to my husband, Kent Putnam, who is the sun in my solar system. He brings light and warmth to my life.

Thank you for your love and support.

The Exclamation Point!

I am here to advocate for the lowly exclamation point. In a world of confusing semicolons, Oxford commas, and quotation marks, the poor exclamation point, as clear and unequivocal as a mark can be, has long been the subject of derision. It is puerile punctuation because enthusiasms are the province of youth.

If you are caught being enthusiastic in an adult poem or writing of any kind, except perhaps a movie poster, you are a callow fellow. No gravitas. Not a greyback. Its critics complain that is over-used. More over-used than a period? Surely that is far and away the most used mark of punctuation. The simple, or maybe not so simple declarative sentence. Full stop.

I have not one thing against the period. In fact, I have no feelings about punctuation at all. I consider it a necessary part of language to more fully communicate. You know commas are brilliant at that. They may be the most used punctuation. They are the navigators of written language. The heroes of the written word. "Let's eat Grandma" and "Let's eat, Grandma" are very different sentences. I personally see nothing wrong with putting an exclamation point at the end of each of those sentences, no matter how grandma turns out.

Eating is an enthusiasm at my house. Perhaps the exclamation point became a second-class punctuation because middle school girls tend to use it to express their boundless glee and excitement. If one exclamation point is delighted, four exclamation points is over the moon. A hundred of them is a serious crush on that boy in algebra class. I get that. I mean one cannot misuse the period. What is there after full stop?

Okay, the multiple question mark is sometimes used to show not just a simple interrogatory but deep confusion or sarcasm. My personal punctuation horror is the ellipsis. All those dangling periods indicating an unfinished thought. No. It is three dots, space, period. But no one but me gives a hoot. No one snidely remarks on the use of ellipsis. Dot, dot, dot, dot, dot, dot, dot.

One of my favorite poets announced the other day that he was going back and removing all the exclamation points from his poems. I was put in mind of Oscar Wilde working all day to decide if a comma should be in or out. Punctuation is critical. I get it. But the exclamation point genocide is a step too far.

An Existential Question

I have two grandsons, Gavin, the older, and Beckett. They are about seventeen months apart, and do not share a single scrap of DNA, an allele, a commonality with me. They are the children of my husband's daughter. Said daughter is the offspring of a fabulous mother who is the role model for the daughter's own fabulous mothering. I got a great package deal when I married him.

The boys were born after their grandmother's death, and I am the only Bubby they have ever known. Yes, they also have a paternal Granny, but that is an entirely different thing. When you get married, you might possibly be young enough to think you are just getting a spouse. One more bell to answer, one more egg to fry, as the song goes. No. Only if you are marrying someone in the witness protection program. In all other cases, you get his friends who hopefully become your friends. You get his enemies who you never liked anyway. You get his family, the parents, the siblings, the failure to launch younger brother and the sixth marriage-is a-charm sister. And you get his children. And any children of the children that might come along. It is a pyramid scheme of the most sinister proportions, and you only realize how totally you have been had when a tiny hand grasps yours, looks down at his damp shoes and says, I need to pee.

So it was that Gavin, who was about four and had six elbows and six knees, all firmly wedged into my soft body in various inhumane ways, was snuggled into me, and we were looking at family pictures and he was naming all his relatives for me.

Smart boy! We had flipped through several pictures when he suddenly sat up straight and said, "Bubby! Where is Beckett?"

I loved this question. Isn't it the third or fourth child who is supposed to notice that his older sibs have far more pictures than he does? Here was number one child looking for number two. "Beckett had not been born yet," I explained.

"Oh. But where was he?"

"He had not been born yet when the pictures were taken," I stupidly repeated.

"I know, Bubby, I know. But where was he?"

I looked at him. What a sophisticated question for a four-year-old. "Gav, Beckett did not yet exist yet as Beckett, but all his parts were ready in Mommy and Daddy and in you. All three of you made the Beckett we have now."

He considered this. I held my breath. "Cool," he said.

So why can't I just let this go? Why does the question of where was Beckett before he was born drift around in my head bumping in and out of consciousness? I think there was a Peanuts cartoon in which Lucy screams to Charlie Brown, "I wish you'd never been born!"

And he thinks, *The theological implications alone are staggering.* Can a four-year-old be an existentialist?

Covid Chronicles 7: 5/21/20

I am still hunkered down in our home. I do not leave the house. Our groceries are still delivered to the end of our driveway, and we bring them in and wipe them down with disinfectant. All of our social life is suspended. Friends get "together" on Zoom for chats and to maintain contact. We can only see our grandchildren online. The quarantine is isolating.

At least there are two of us. I really cannot imagine how people who live alone are managing. There is no school, and parents working from home, those still lucky enough to have jobs, are also tasked with homeschooling their children. Graduating seniors will have no proms and no graduation ceremonies. This is not easy. Still, I thought, this is America. We rise to challenges and eat up difficulties as if they were gumdrops. We can do this!

I barely recognize my fellow Americans. The state capital of Michigan was swarmed with people carrying assault weapons and wearing MAGA hats. They did not want their governor to extend the time of the shut-down. They carried American flags and screamed into the faces of the cops standing in a cordon to keep them from entering the legislative chambers. Their position is that it is their body, and if they want to risk getting sick, it is their right under the Constitution to do so. Their body, their choice. [I do not remember that provision, and that was not their position when the issue was abortion.] Their right to scream obscenities presumptively protected by the First Amendment, their right to open carry assault weapons on legislative grounds, all presumptively protected by the

Second Amendment. "Give me liberty or give me death!" they screamed. "Don't tread on me!" All evoking a very different United States than this Spring of 2020.

They are deaf to the issue of spreading the virus to people who are vulnerable. It is happening all over the country. Protestors demanding that everything be "normalized". It is about the economy. They are broke. They have no jobs and no money. One in six is unemployed. But the only idea that the protesters have is to try and put the genie back in the bottle. "Open everything up! We'd rather be dead than broke!" Well, they would rather I be dead than they be broke. [The most detestable words in any language: S/he has lived a good, long life. And therefore, long lives are expendable.] The protestors have big guns to underscore their argument. Bullies.

Guns have been selling like hotcakes. Who are these people going to shoot? Who is coming after them with guns? Not the government they hate, that government as represented by Trump says they are all good people who are just angry. He encourages this behavior. "Liberate Michigan," he tweeted. Liberate any state not opening on the time schedule he prefers for "opening up" the economy. These rioters are supported by the very government they want to bring down.

What, I can only wonder, would that do to the economy? A revolution at the time we are trying to survive a pandemic with the revolutionaries cheered on by their President. Could anyone even write this doomsday script? 1,000 people died of Corona virus yesterday in the state of Georgia. I live about fifteen miles from the Georgia border. Their governor, who initially thought he was complying with the Trump timeline, allowed the shutdown to be weakened yesterday. Significantly. Trump said it was too soon. Our own governor did the same thing two days later, but after visiting with Trump. His moves apparently are approved.

Can this be the same nation that went to World War II totally unprepared, endured years of rationing, huge changes in our society, and lost thousands of men and women? No. It is not. That generation is almost entirely gone. What is left cannot apparently endure a three- or four-month quarantine.

Where are the innovators redirecting our economy? Where are the thinkers, the planners, the clever souls who know that 2019 is dead and gone and 2020 and 2021 will require a whole new rule book? All those people who were on ventilators will require special services.

Our farmers need immediate help and intervention if our nation is not going to starve. Why aren't we talking about harvesting the food, storing it, getting it to stores and to food banks? Why are we not talking right now how people will be inoculated once we have a vaccine? Who will have priority? How will this proceed? It cannot be as ephemeral as the promise of tests for this disease turned out to be. Where are our planners, our thinkers?

Sadly, we know they are not anywhere near our President. His enclave of incompetents blunders from day to day, never thinking that they are not up to any single task. We were once smart enough to, say, find the best minds in the country and put them on this problem. Now it all has to do with slavish obedience to a very limited man.

The one bright star in this dark universe has been our first responders: The doctors, nurses, medical staff that have put their own health and families at risk to work to exhaustion to save lives.

I am afraid. I am afraid of losing my country. I am afraid of losing my life. I am afraid that my neighbors are not who I thought they were. I am afraid for the people I love, for my friends, for my family. This is America with all the rainbows stripped from our eyes.

Falling

I fell today. Not quite sure what happened. Was I conscious when I fell? I think I was.

At first, it was slow motion and I thought I could right myself. Then the floor was coming straight for my face very fast, and I was lying on the bedroom floor with my head against a small wooden shelf, dry sobbing.

Not crying. I was not hurt and not in pain. Just terrified at what had just happened. Alone except for Figaro who is not quite big enough to lend a hand. I lay there and took a quick assessment. All limbs working. No scratches or bruises. But how was I going to get off the floor?

Down is always so easy. Thanks, gravity. But up is harder as my age increases. One knee and hip are replaced. They do not like my entire weight resting on them. My left knee has had osteoporosis issues. It cannot be counted on to support me.

I sat up and pulled my gown and robe down over my knees to act as insulation and crawled, sort of, to the side of the bed. I stretched my arms out as far as they would go and, using the bedcovers, pulled myself up. Every single solitary joint complained the entire time. They screamed, "No, no, no, stop this right now!"

I ignored them, and after what felt like Sisyphus rolling his boulder up the mountain, I collapsed on the bed and could sit and stand from there. I resumed dry sobbing because this micro-drama had scared the daylights out of me, and I was just fine.

Now I am working on getting my heart rate back to something like normal. I had no idea old age would be like this. I was oblivious most of my life. Maybe I still am. Now that the adrenalin is returning to status quo, I am sore. That is all. Just sore.

Family

My parents were married for sixty years when my mother died. They told my brothers and me many times that the secret of their long marriage was an agreement early on that the one who asked for the divorce had to take the kids.

Years ago, I watched their grandchildren dancing at their golden wedding anniversary. That was the milestone we celebrated. The fiftieth. Now those grandchildren are married and have their own children. I hope that the memory of their grandparents' commitment will sustain them when their marriages suffer the difficulties that all marriages do. We don't talk much about family values in this family – we just do it.

The whole term "family" has a very free and easy concept with us. When I got a great package deal by marrying a man with children, my family simply added them to the family tree. I don't think blood is thicker than water – if you have blood in your veins, you can be one of us. Even green Vulcan blood. To be one of us, you have to love us back. Our elastic family includes "steps", "adopteds", and relations so attenuated that intermarriage wouldn't be a problem. Tacky – but not a problem.

One year for Father's Day, I adopted a manatee in my dad's name. When the manatee adoption society sent Dad a picture of his manatee son, he hung it on the wall with the rest of the family pictures. The manatee's name is Crazy Nick. He's right up there in the family gallery between Marty and Larry, my brothers.

This is a society that teaches love as a competitive sport. Step-mothers vs. mothers, step-fathers vs. fathers, mothers vs. fathers. Our family believes that you cannot be loved by too many people, and that loving one person does not reduce the available love you have to give to another.

We've slogged through several generations with those simplistic ideas. Married, mutually committed, for sixty and more years. Easy does it.

Family Zoom

Thanks to Covid, we have something we call Family Zoom initiated and gently guided by our "matriarch", Shirley. We have been doing this for at least a year, perhaps longer, and I just love it. There are still fourteen of the original seventeen first cousins living. We are the offspring of six siblings. We all share the grandparents on that side of the family.

Now the cousins' children and grandchildren are on this family Zoom. Here is what I have noticed: Not a single criticism. Ever. Lots of mutual support, attaboys, laughter, cheers. It is hard to get a word in edgewise because we are talkers.

Yesterday, we kept saying we needed to get off after an hour or so but kept on talking for another hour. One of the topics yesterday was Levittisms, those words that only our family uses. Were they from Russian? Lithuanian? Yiddish? Somehow, that morphed into stories about children being put down a laundry chute by their brother and sister.

This is my favorite story from yesterday: Scott Michalove, Shirley's son, has a largely gifted [they were given to him] collection of Mr. Potato Heads. This began when he was in college and had a carrel in the library which he marked as his own with a Mr. Potato Head. One day, he came in and Mr. Potato Head was gone! In his place was a note made from letters cut from a magazine demanding payment for Mr. Potato Head's return.

I do not remember what the payment was, it does not matter, Scott said no. He made flyers showing a picture of Mr. Potato Head and offering an award for information leading to his safe return and posted them all over campus. He received an additional note with Mr. Potato Head's ear. Then an additional note with a picture of a large baked potato. Then a note with a large serving of French fries. All letters cut from magazines.

Finally, Mr. Potato Head was returned with his hands tied behind his back, his eyes blindfolded. Scott put a band-aid where his ear had been. He still has it. Showed us. Great laughter.

Over these months, people have dropped in and dropped out. The people who stay are the four Krick cousins, and their children and grandchildren. I am there. But our older cousins do not come. Our younger cousins do not come. Larry's sons and grandchildren have largely drifted away, but they at least came for a short while. My brother, Marty, never comes, and neither do his daughters. They are missing these hilarious stories from our youth that really show who we are. And I mean we in the largest sense.

We live on both coasts and in England. Zoom keeps us closer than we would have otherwise been. We only saw one another as adults at funerals as each of those six sibs and their spouses died. Even weddings and bar mitzvahs were no longer required attendance.

So, I thank my cousin Shirley, Scott, Zoom, and all my relatives, no matter how attenuated, for showing up once a month for a little family anthropology. I had an anthropology book in college that said, "Culture is spread by intercourse among friendly hordes." I swear to God.

Feast of Words

My grandmother, watching Khrushchev and his famous shoe pounding address to the UN from the removed safety of our living room TV, responded in furious Russian, shook her fist, and admonished my father to protect his watching children from contamination.

My father, in turn, argued aloud to TV editorials, sniped ongoingly at the oblivious news correspondent, and at one time was so furious with various editorial writers in the newspapers in his area that there were no more acceptable newspapers for my parents to read.

Watching the news in our house is an interactive experience and was long before computer software and other gadgets allowed less unrestrained families to click their responses with mouse and icons. At our place, the news (really any program, but particularly the news) is a springboard for opinions, all strongly held, all forcefully argued. If there are five of us in the room, there will be at least six opinions. Not counting the oblivious talking head.

My spouse fit right in with this group. His specialty was playing devil's advocate. We learned over the years that acquaintances found us intense, opinionated, argumentative. We were dismayed that many found these to be disturbing, negative, even pejorative qualities. A good friend who has shared many meals with us over the years commented that she loved to watch us fight.

"Fight?" I asked. What was she talking about?

"Oh, it was always about some principle, capital punishment or something. It was like watching a tennis game," she said.

I was nonplussed. That's not fighting, that's making love. This is sharing of yourself in a most intimate way. It is an open book, non-secretive way to live. We find those who sidestep issues fundamentally untrustworthy. Who knows how they really feel? And they think so little of our thinking processes that they are unwilling to hone them in verbal steel-on-stone clashes.

We never have lulls in conversations at our house. We even talk in our sleep. But we especially talk, and yes, argue, at the table. Our daughter calls this prandial patter "trial by brunch," at which the unsuspecting are dropped into the cauldron of boiling opinion.

I call it a feast of words.

Feet

My parents moved us to Japan just ten years after the end of World War II. To a country that had bombed Pearl Harbor mercilessly and demonstrated its ferocity throughout the Pacific and Asia, my parents moved three children, a cocker spaniel and their red and white '54 Chevy. My brothers were two and eight. I was ten. None of us children had any thought that Japan had been an enemy; that we might be hated, or that we had any reason to be hateful. To us, it was just life as usual: one more stop in the parade across the globe that my father had chosen for our lives. My mother made inquiry as to whether we might need to pack mosquito netting.

We left Hutchinson, Kansas, a place as beige and drear as any place we'd ever lived, to travel across the American West in that red and white Chevy. Arriving finally in San Francisco, my parents loaded three children, dog and car onto the *Gaffey*, a Military Sea Transport Service ship full of military men headed for posts across the Pacific. With no sense of irony or foreboding, we sailed for Hawaii on a June day in 1955. After a brief stopover, it was on to Japan.

I will never forget my first glimpse of this magical island. This was not the Japan of Sony, Panasonic, Toyota and Honda. In fact, from the distance of 1955, those now commonplace realities seemed flatly impossible. It was raining gently as we docked at a place where nearly naked Japanese men wearing bamboo hats and rain capes with a sort of breech cloth were busily loading, unloading and storing packages in large warehouses. Japan was so green, it seemed to shimmer in the rain. It took my breath away.

The green hydrated our eyes, revived them, and the beige and dust of Kansas dissolved. My mother quietly placed her hand on my shoulder as we drank in the splendor that was to be our home. Mt. Fuji rose blue, symmetrically perfect and still capped with snow.

If Japan looked exotic to us, we must have seemed like aliens from hell to the Japanese. It wasn't just that we were so obviously foreign in a notoriously xenophobic society – we were huge, outsize foreigners.

Crowds gathered around my 6'4" father. When we went to buy shoes, the shoe salesman gathered his friends and family to gaze in wonder at the size of my dad's feet. The Japanese gaped, pointed and laughed. Dad could have been insulted, angry. Instead, he looked at those long, thin feet too, and joined in the great joke of how many sizes and shapes we humans come in. He looked at himself through their eyes.

My parents took us to a place of old enemies without warning, without prejudice or bigotry. This was the country of the Japanese. We let Japan happen to us, and it was wonderful. My parents wanted our experiences to teach us. They did.

My parents were sort of reverse missionaries, letting the world bring its message to us. In the wake of the travel ban, in a time of powder keg religious zealotry and the revival of ancient tribal identities, I wish my parents could pack a bunch of these xenophobes off to a small village to shop for shoes. We could all use a good laugh at our feet.

Fifteen, and Counting

Tomorrow Kent Putnam and I will be married to one another for fifteen years. I have to add that "to one another" because this is not the first rodeo for either of us. And please spare me your "we've been married forty-eight, fifty-four, whatever number of years." You are bloody lucky that the spouse who was the center of your universe did not die after a paltry thirty-two years. So quit bragging.

I married Kent when I was sixty years old. The person I was at sixty had a lot, a huge lot, to do with being married to Harry Walborsky for more than half of my adult life. My identity was not Paula Levitt. It was Paula Walborsky. That is who Harry Walborsky created with his love and support, his craziness, his past, his wonderful stories, his love of travel, his long, excruciating years of global aphasia. My adult memories all featured Harry. My ideas about how to celebrate holidays, and which holidays to celebrate, all had to do with my life with Harry. The very concept, the very definition of what a spouse was, what their duties and joys were was inflected by Harry Walborsky. From age twenty-four until fifty-six is a big chunk of a human's life. We two had become one.

As I have said many times before, once you have been happily married, all you want to be is happily married. Somehow, some part of me wanted to be married. Neither of us wanted to be alone. Can you imagine the risk Kent was taking? The risk I was taking? This marriage would require us to reinvent ourselves. At age sixty, that is no small order. We had to create a new we. A Walborsky-Putnam we.

So, what makes a married we? If you are in your twenties, which was about par for our generation's marriage time, you could anticipate two sets of live parents, the likelihood of children, career choices and growth, graduate school or more study. A first trip together to Europe, the car trip with the kids, the first house, the first pet you both selected. The best friends who became your steadies for double dates. The gradual loss of parents and grandparents, perhaps moving to a place where the only people you know are one another.

In short, if you are lucky, you have a lifetime of shared history to make. We had done that. With someone else.

But everything was better with Kent. We loved the same music, knew all the words, sang out loud and hilariously. We loved little theater and big theater, movies, musicals, just driving around in the car. Playing cribbage. He admired my gardening. I admired his photography. We are both secretly *Jeopardy* champions. He and my brother are great; I get on swimmingly with his sister. We like the same food, and he likes my cooking.

And then our grandsons were born. I know there was love and anxiety and exhaustion in the world before there were grandchildren. But what was the point? We read to them every night. They are the best of all those combined genes and are the one and only champions of all things in their weight classes. I did not know you could love someone this way until they were born.

I never had a plan of growing old. My plan sort of petered out at end career and retire. Then what? All of this time, all these wonderfully unplanned and unanticipated days are for Kent and me to live together. He walks and hikes, I go to water aerobics and swimming. We are committed to taking care of ourselves and one another. If one of us is ill or gimpy, it affects both of us. We say to one another, "I love my life. Thank you."

If only I could become a sports fan.

Figaro

Living with cats is an adventure. We are staff to a quite large tuxedo cat named Figaro. He weighs about twenty pounds and is not fat. He walks with a swagger and pretty much anticipates that the world and everything in it are under his dominion. He has his own doors to the great outside, and he visits his realm daily. Sometimes he comes right back in, and at others he walks about, checking the furthest reaches of his kingdom. But one thing he likes to do is participate in daily bedmaking.

There are two kinds of people in the world. There are the make-the-bed-daily kind and the what-the-hell-we-are-just-going-to-sleep-in-it-again-tonight kind. Intermarriage should be forbidden. Luckily, Kent and I are the same kind: Daily bed makers. He gets on his side, I on mine, and in about three minutes, the bed is once again neatly made. I mean, what if the bed-making police happened by and discovered our bed, covers gaping open, wrinkled, and unmade? Unacceptable. Two type A's that found one another.

Often, after his breakfast, Figaro returns to our bed for a nap until his lunch time. We have tried gently removing him from the bed so that we can make it. He just gets back in. Often faster than I can stand up. So, we make the bed around him. Giving ourselves additional points for difficulty in the cutthroat competition for best bed making. We say, and now with a difficulty of 9.8, the team of Putnam and Walborsky approach the bed with large, sleeping cat dead center. Pulling the covers up can be a challenge with a twenty-pound cat on them.

We get it done, check that it is lumpless [except for the cat] and smooth, and give ourselves full points for sticking the landing. Even the East German judge is impressed. We advance to the finals.

First Show

When I was sixteen, my maternal grandmother took me to see my first Broadway show. She liked to go up to New York each year for a couple of days crammed with shows, good food, great shopping. Her brother, who lived in New York City, got the tickets, and they were waiting at the will call window. We were living at the time in Annandale, Virginia, just outside Washington, D.C. This was some silent acknowledgement that I was old enough to accompany my testy grandmother.

My boyfriend of that era, Roger Goldstein, lived across the street from me, and he was entertaining another young woman who, with her mother, were visiting the Goldsteins. Jealous? You have no idea. I was "eat up with it", as they say. So, it was a good time to get out of town anyway.

The show we saw was "Camelot". King Arthur was played by Richard Burton, Julie Andrews was Guinevere, Robert Goulet was Lancelot, Roddy McDowell was Mordred. Yes. I truly hit the jackpot. But I did not know it yet. The theater was rather small, and when the lights went down, my whole spirit started to glow with a strange new intensity that just crescendoed when Robert Goulet walked to the front of an otherwise empty stage to sing "C'est Moi". The libretto to Camelot is very smart, very funny, and tender by turns. Lancelot knows he should be modest, but to undersell his gifts, his prowess, would be to lie. I was literally on the edge of my seat.

Mt grandmother had no need to ask if I liked "Camelot". I suggested we turn in our other tickets and just watch four more productions of "Camelot". I wanted to stay fixed to my seat. It was such a wonderful experience.

After the show, we went to dinner and enthused to one another about the clever lyrics, the wonderful acting. I bought a record of the cast singing their songs, and I still have it. Surely, I have listened to it a hundred times, tummy down on the rug in front of the hi-fi in the living room. I don't think I can choose a favorite song, but of course, this was just a year before President Kennedy was assassinated, and the song Richard Burton sings, "Camelot", where it only rains after sundown and by 9PM, the moonlight must appear, has always been the choice to encapsulate that time of hope and grace for our country.

We did see other plays on that trip. I do not remember them. We ate at some fancy shmancy restaurants and shopped at huge department stores. They are all lost to time and age. But I think I can still sing every word, every nuance of "Camelot", and in my mind, I see Julie Andrews asking if she should not have the simple joys of maidenhood, maybe start a little war, and Richard Burton asking, "What do the simple folk do when they are feeling blue?" To my often-impossible grandmother, thank you a million times over. I am still enjoying that show sixty years later.

The First Time

My husband had bought the house we lived in a couple of years before we met and married. It was not a beautiful house. There was worn linoleum in the kitchen, and the windows at the side of the kitchen looked out on the carport. Why would anyone want a view of a carport?

He lived there with his two teenaged sons, and the house was full of taxidermied fish and souvenirs from bull fights. There was a full bar with the skin of some large cat tacked above it. It would have been appropriate if you had to enter by climbing a rope ladder. It also had a full-sized pool table and an outdoor pool that had only been the home of catfish. And a small gun rack.

My mom visited us just before we got married. This was a woman who had made one home after another from whatever we could find to rent on Dad's travels. She looked around and said, "Where are you going to live after you get married?"

"Here," I said.

"Oh, Honey, good luck," she replied.

Outside the house, there was lawn and more lawn. And around the pool, there was a fence topped with barbed wire. None of those catfish were going anywhere. I started outside. Clearly, no one much cared about the outside.

I started reading gardening books, one after another, filling my head with dreams of gardens of flowers. I realized after I had killed bulbs and roses and flowers from seed that 'full sun' means 'full sun' in Massachusetts, New Hampshire. Full sun in Florida is a weapon of mass vegetation destruction. Had there been an organization against cruelty to green things, I would have been arrested many times over.

I talked with Mr. Nesmith who had a nursery out Thomasville Road, and to Gene Ellis of Tallahassee Nurseries, and Mrs. Rosa of Rosa's Daylilies. They were so very kind and patient and gave me their time and expertise. What a wonderful community we have.

When I wanted to try day lilies, Mrs. Rosa would not sell them to me until I had prepared the earth to receive them. "You have to put a little bit of goody in each hole," she instructed. And I went home and prepared the garden and put a bit of the fertilizer she recommended in each hole. THEN and only then, we talked about which daylilies to choose. She was so smart about all things botany and gardening. A one-woman reference library.

An older husband comes with older friends. Those lovely women gave me cuttings and advice on what works in Tallahassee and what doesn't. No matter how much you love peonies, they do not grow here. Same with lilac. But I discovered gingers and my beloved gloriosa lily Rothschildeana. Gorgeously flamboyant. And azaleas! Lots and lots of azaleas and camellias and sasanquas. Every weekend, I was outside tearing out lawns and putting in flower beds. The first thing to go was the fence around the pool. The yard was completely fenced in any case. This was just an eyesore.

I convinced Harry to knock out the whole back wall of the house and open it to the pool and gardens in the back. He loved it. We put in patios and pergolas and grew kiwi vines, grapes and wisteria. We invented shade, and grass hates shade and began to die back. I made more and more gardens. We had less and less grass.

If you were the person who had to cut the grass [not I] in Tallahassee's heat and humidity, the less grass the better. Forty-one years later, there was no grass to cut.

I put in a floor-to-ceiling window in our family room. It faced south over the hydrangeas, to the crabapple tree and the azaleas. A long pergola of kiwi grew there. I often hung big baskets of flowers from that pergola.

One night, dressed only in my nightgown, I went outside and started down the steps toward this pergola. My cat, Moneypenny, was being stubborn about coming in. But she bounded up to me, and we turned and went back in. The next morning, I found every one of my hanging baskets on the ground by the pergola. Someone had been with me in the dark as I called for Moneypenny.

Flash Fiction

This is something I heard about from my niece, Rachael, who has an MFA in creative writing, and then from Josephine Yu, a poet who has become something like a friend/daughter/mentor/co-conspirator. I do not write flash fiction, at least not intentionally. When I put it on paper, I think it is the truth. It is what I remember or what I think about something. If anything, it is too truthful. But you need to understand that it is sort of a stand-in for therapy. So is water aerobics. Both are enormously effective. And more affordable than therapy.

As encouragement and a sort of peek into very short prose written by others, Josephine gifted me with two books: *Heating & Cooling* by Beth Ann Fennelly which has what are described as fifty-two micro-memoirs. I gobbled this one up last night, laughing and admiring her style. Some of these are only a line or two long: "Why I'm switching Salons" [title]. "We can put on a topcoat with glitter," said the manicurist. "We've noticed you like attention."

Twenty words, including the must-have title. Twenty perfect, no further exposition required, words. I laughed out loud and, at the same time, wondered, as she must have, *What-the-hell?* Twenty words, two emotions. Not bad. And that is not counting my admiration.

The second book is a compilation of flash fiction originally published in a magazine called Brevity. It is called *Best of*

Brevity and is edited by Zoe Bossiere and Dinty W. Moore. These are nothing short of amazing. *Poster Children* by Sandra Gail Lambert gave me chills. It is all of two and a half pages long. It is the story of severely handicapped protestors, ADAPT, disability rights activists who are jailed.

These are so good. Each a small marvel. So brilliantly crafted.

The thing about long books is that you can get deliciously submerged in them. I have climbed out of the depths of some of my favorites speaking like the characters. I have cried when the ending was not what I wanted. I have been unendurable when an author and I agree on the perfect ending. So, I understand the delight in sagas, trilogies, the book so long it is hard to read in bed because of its weight.

Reading these literate bon-bons is like an evening with a good friend. There is story-telling, a sharing of insights, an admiration of the teller. One does not have to choose. You can read both long and short. Perhaps you have not tried these very short stories, or memoir, however. I had not. I recommend them to you. Both thumbs way up.

Covid Chronicles 8: A Covid Calendar: 6/28/20

For all the years we are married, my husband and I have kept a New Yorker calendar of the year. I save them, and we can see when we went to Jacksonville two years ago to see Equus, when we had dinner with our dear friends the Yus, when Kent had a showing of his photography. They are both reminders of what is coming and a journal of what we did.

Not realizing that 2020 would be a year of no gatherings and isolation, we bought one for this year, too. In March, around Kent's birthday on the eighteenth, it takes a somber turn. His birthday party is canceled. Our trips to see our grandchildren were canceled. Our life outside our safe four walls – canceled. But recently, I have noticed the pages filling up again as we learn to accommodate the need to stay isolated. Here is what it looks like now:

My beloved water aerobics classes are canceled. Now, every morning, I go for a swim at the very carefully monitored public pool. I call for an appointment and am assigned a specific lane. I swim for an hour and soak up the vitamin D and let my endorphins run wild. Kent gave me a Syryn which is an MP3 player that is waterproof. I get in the water and workout to my music.

Kent's gym is closed. Every morning, Kent walks at least three miles in one of our many state and federal parks. Or just a wide loop around our neighborhood. Sometimes he brings his camera, sometimes he does not. Sometimes he rides his bike instead. And for at least an hour, he too cranks up the endorphins and gathers in the natural vitamin D. His only day of rest is Sunday. Often his routine is followed by a workout at home with weights. Figaro supervises.

We both belong to book clubs that Zoom once a month. Those meetings are about two hours long. Sometimes more.

We both have "conference" calls with friends. Kent calls the Freds every two weeks. The Freds travel together and have been friends since at least middle school. They are Kent's brothers by another mother. This connection is deeply important. These calls can easily run over an hour or more.

I am one on a conference call with three other former bridge buddies and friends. Weekly, we talk about our lives, politics, our health, books, TV, memories. Our bridge games were a bit more disciplined than this. I cherish this call every Tuesday morning. What amazing women. I would like to add that some of the people on this call are Democrats, and some are life-long Republicans. None is a Trump supporter. But I listen to what these smart people have to say. This call usually lasts about an hour.

On Tuesday, I also talk with two friends from high school, Roger Goldstein and Judith Claremon. They live in Utah and Arizona, so their daily lives are much different from mine. We talk about the weather, Roger's DIY projects, Judith's Justice Circles, our grandchildren, politics, what we are reading, the occasional movie. They are my connection to my childhood. And my first loves.

Tuesday night is a treat to ourselves. I DON'T COOK! We belong to something called The Tuesday Night Supper Club started by Lucilla's restaurant to get them and us through the isolation. They post a monthly menu of what they will be bringing right to our door for us. It is delivered by a man or woman wearing a mask. Everything is heated to 450 degrees before eaten. It is varied and delicious. And did I mention I don't have to cook it? Yes! We get out the good dishes and make an event out of it. Yay, Tuesday night.

So, Tuesday is our "busy" day.

On Thursday, I order groceries from Publix that will be delivered to my driveway at a time I choose by Instacart. We bring the bags in once the delivery person drives away. Not a perfect system, but it keeps me out of the grocery stores where some have decided to die on the hill of not wearing a mask.

On Friday, I have a 7AM Zoom with friends from our 7AM water aerobics class. I do not know how many years we have seen one another almost every morning in class. Occasionally we went for coffee or had lunch together, laughing that we barely recognized one another in real clothes. Now, we occasionally run into one another at the pool, our appointments coincidentally overlapping. And we gather on Zoom on Friday morning and catch up. I miss them and the fun we had in class.

Both Kent and I belong to book clubs that meet once a month on Fridays. Now on Zoom. Not a terrible way to have a book club. But I miss the actual presence of my friends. I miss being in their homes. I miss my life.

Flash Mob

Forgive my bragging: David Krick is my cousin. His mom and my dad were siblings. I have shamelessly written about David in the past because David is an altruist. You may not know this word as we live in a Capitalist society [capital C], and it is a dying concept. David lives his life doing mitzvahs, kindnesses for others, and expecting no give back, no return on his investment of time and money. Except the joy of it.

We are two of seventeen first cousins, so we really did not connect until we were in our forties. My husband had a catastrophic stroke, and suddenly my mailbox was full of funny items David had discovered in his ramblings around Key West, there were notes, cards, plastic Yoda cups. He kept it up to this very day, and a loving, affectionate relationship was born. He sends gifts to my cat, Figaro, sends fancy foods, funny tee shirts, books of lawyer jokes, you name it. He also sends his sibs and me links to wonderful things he finds on the interwebs. This morning, it was a flash mob in Antwerp.

This got me to thinking. I just love the idea of public spaces being taken over on surprise occasions for music, dance, singing. The unexpectedness of it, a rail station suddenly filled with people laughing and singing, dancing in a place of people who usually have their heads down to their devices. A mall, a plaza, a thoroughfare, once anonymous, everyone very carefully not making eye contact with anyone else. Distance as civilized behavior gives way to the synchronous joy of singing, dancing, making music. From our stone canyons comes delight. Children applaud, people grin, lots of recordings fill up those devices.

David is himself a one-man flash mob. The grimmer that lonely plaza inside you, the greater the delight in his unexpected gifts. Going through life with David is a joy shared. Along the way, he holds up his finds for us to enjoy. He is fun personified. Kindness and, yes, altruism are his biggest character traits. He shows up in your dark, lights a hundred candles, tells three terrible jokes and gives your cat addictive catnip. He is a giver of light. He is a giver. A one-man flash mob giver. Forgive my bragging.

Flowers For Algernon

Do you remember this story? Algernon is a lab rat who gets smarter and smarter after experimental brain surgery, but then there is a reversal, and all he learned, all he accomplished, fell away. He died. A man who had been in the same study as Algernon, Charlie, has the same surgery. He got smarter and smarter until it reversed. He knew what was coming because he had observed Algernon. He finally asks if he can put flowers on Algernon's grave. I feel as if I am living my life like Algernon.

Really, I never considered myself more than average at anything. My mother would remark that I worked hard for my A's. She was right. I pushed myself and took lots of classes because I wanted to be smarter. At least better educated. I still take classes. But I find that subjects I knew well, things I worked hard to acquire, are falling away.

One can say this is just a symptom of aging, but I feel like Algernon and his human lab rat. That others suffer the same losses, and more, does not comfort me at all. What a cold comfort that would be.

The wrinkles, grey hair, the arthritis, the death of my metabolism and libido I can bear, grudgingly. It is the cost of aging for most living things. If you die young, you can look better in an open casket funeral. The loss of my memory, the inability to distinguish faces, the wretched confusion that sneaks into the easiest exercise, those are the killers of self-worth and confidence, the vanquishers of self-esteem.

I have friends older than I am by a decade and more. They claim that they too have moments when they cannot remember why they are standing in the kitchen. Did they take a pill? Is the day Thursday or Wednesday? We laugh about these reveals. But where will it all end? We all know.

So, I have to ask. Have I written this essay before?

Forgiveness

The concept of forgiveness is very difficult to me. Every Yom Kippur, I am to ask forgiveness of the people around me for my transgressions and ask God for His forgiveness. God, I suppose will deny me forgiveness if I have not sought forgiveness from my family and friends. So, what kind of faux forgiveness is that? So, I am surely being too literal. It means go into the new year without the weights, the disappointments of the current year. Begin anew. Eat apples and honey, and aim for sweetness in your life. It does not matter what religion you are. Forgiveness is a part of it.

I cannot get there from here.

What about justice? You have seen the phrase, if you want peace, work for justice. That resonates with me. I am firmly convinced that it is the job of adults to be judgmental. Life's experience, education, they are all brought to bear in judgement.

There have been articles written about people who have forgiven their child's murderer. Visit him in jail, work for his release. I am gobsmacked. I think of myself as a gentle person, but lay one finger on my husband, brother, people I love, and I promise retribution. I may have to settle for justice, but I can guarantee you nothing like forgiveness will bloom in this raggedy old body. Not ever. There are some things that are just unforgiveable.

Intent, motive play their part. Justice must be hammered out in each individual case. Each fact of the case helps to form what kind of justice is necessary. Justice, unlike forgiveness, is not one size fits all. But justice, the quid for your quo is more essential, more part of the human psyche than forgiveness.

Shall I forgive people who have caused me pain? Why would I do that? And if a friend, a loved one has caused you pain, what happened to the trust that was an essential part of that relationship? Can one have a close relationship without trust? Surely just a civil countenance is all that is required. Or maybe I am just an old curmudgeon sick to death of the unkindness, the murderous volatility of our species.

Franklin and Eleanor

My husband was away on a business trip when I wandered into a pet shop and admired the peach-faced love birds. The store owner sidled over and told me in tones that suggested he also sold drugs on the street that he'd sell the pair to me for half price and throw in the cage for free if I'd take them with me immediately.

"What's wrong with them?" I asked, surveying their obviously healthy, chunky green bodies and rosy faces.

"Oh, not a thing," the owner assured me. "They are perfectly healthy. Just can't keep them in the cage. Every night, they not only get out, but then liberate every other bird in the place. They are creating chaos."

My first thought was that this offer was: One, timely – Harry was away and not available to assert his good sense; and Two, I had no other birds to liberate, so what harm could they do? And Three, what a deal!

I put the birds and their large cage in a room full of special plants. Forewarned about their Houdini antics, I secured the door of their cage with both a metal bread twist and a plastic strip used to close heavy garbage bags. I named them Franklin and Eleanor and went to sleep, delighted with my beautiful acquisitions.

The next morning, they were both out of the cage. They had amused themselves by systematically pulling the leaves off the plants and by discovering a mirror in the bathroom. The mirror had a wood trim, and they were busily biting pieces out of it, chewing the wood into a wad of goop, and then affixing goop to the mirror. From the look of things, they had been at work for hours.

On successive nights, I tried rope, string, fishing line and bent paper clips. Harry came home and suggested there was some poetic justice in all this. Then, one morning several months later, we found Eleanor dead in the cage. Her perfect little green and rose body showed no sign of injury – though Harry swore he saw beak marks and said that Franklin had killed Eleanor because she was such a raucous shrew. (She was a bit loud.)

Franklin redoubled his escape attempts. We finally resorted to one of those small padlocks that are used on luggage to give travelers a false sense of security. We were so convinced that we had finally won, that when the weather turned warm, we hung Franklin's cage outside under the arbor. An hour later, he was out of the cage. All day long, I despaired that I had lost my beautiful green demon.

That night, as it grew quite dark, Franklin flew back into his cage and closed the door behind him. We couldn't believe it. Our prodigal son had returned.

Next morning, Franklin was up and out with the sun. He mostly stayed in the arbor, but sometimes he'd fly around to the front of the house and appear at my wild bird feeder at the kitchen window. The cardinals and jays gave him wide berth.

He did however, take up with a flicker. I think Franklin thought the flicker was a kindred soul. I'd see the flicker fly to a pine bough with Franklin in hot pursuit. The flicker would shoot him nervous little glances while Franklin advanced on him (her?) down the bough, one hop at a time. As soon as

Franklin got too close, the flicker would fly off again. And each night, Franklin would fly into his cage, close the door behind him and settle down for the night.

This worked very well for years. In the winter, Franklin stayed in the house, happy to crawl all over the outside of his cage. In the warmer months, he vacationed in the backyard, made new friends, made surprise visits to our neighbors. Finally, Franklin was happy, and we were happy.

Then, one summer day, one of those sudden thunderstorms hit. Franklin had experienced these before and usually just quickly flew home to the dry security of his cage. We will never know what happened. Whether some flicker had led him too far afield, or whether some bird of prey had decided to try green lovebird for an hors d'oeuvre. Or maybe he became disoriented in the sudden storm. For months, I would rush outside, convinced I had heard his voice. My eyes would scan every branch of every tree hungry for the sight of him.

Franklin was one-of-a-kind who paid us the highest compliment of choosing our home when all the world was open to him.

Fremont, Ohio

My first teaching job was in Fremont, Ohio. Fifteen three-year olds from a local Mexican migrant camp filled my Head Start class. There were never more beautiful children. They were all shiny black hair and laughing eyes. Sadly, their camps had no running water, no electricity, and tuberculosis shared the small shacks with them. In my class, two of the kids had active TB.

Because it was summertime and hot, and because it was an earlier, more innocent time, we battled the TB and the lack of running water by bathing and shampooing the kids at school. On deeply hot Ohio afternoons, we'd set up a sprinkler on the front lawn of the school, strip the kids to their panties and turn them loose. Of course, some didn't have underwear, which is why there's a picture of me in a bathing suit, running and laughing amid a lot of young, wet, naked bodies.

The children loved it. No-tears baby shampoo and sponges in the shapes of fruit added to the fun. After brushing fifteen sets of tiny baby teeth, my aide and I would settle them down on the floor of our classroom – each on his own nap mat – for that delicious kind of sleep that only comes after a good lunch, playing in the sun, and having your back rubbed. Not one of my charges had lice or impetigo which so frequently afflicted the children in the camps.

I could only work this "cleanliness-is-next-to-godliness," however, when the children showed up. They did not show up when the stoop crops, the cucumbers and tomatoes, were ripe for picking. It is easier on the three-year-old, closer to the ground and with the flexibility of youth, to pick stoop crops than exhausted parents. When they finally were returned to me, they were dirty and so tired that one or more would fall asleep while eating lunch.

I would cry with frustration at the return-to-zero pointlessness of it all. But those pint-sized campesinos never gave up. Their resilience, their youth, bounced them back to aspiring, dancing cherubs on the school's broad green lawn. They were born with almost no chance in life. But they took each day as it came, and hard work or hard play, at three, they were already survivors.

Friday

Friday arrived right on time. I remember weeks when I was practicing law when I thought Friday would never arrive. That somewhere around Tuesday or Wednesday it was decided that those days would be 40 hours long. That Friday kept receding into the timeline. But happily, retired as I am, it showed up just when I expected it. TGIF has no real meaning anymore. If I wake up on the right side of the grass, it is a good day. Hell, if I wake up, it is a good day.

My day started with a Zoom to a friend who is attending law school at NYU. We have been doing a 7AM Zoom since she left the 7AM water aerobics class to attend. For a while, several of us joined in this Zoom. But one by one, the others have dropped out, and it has been just me and Mac for quite some time now. I find I tell her things I don't tell other people. I really cherish this friendship.

When she lived in Tallahassee, we always said hi, but we were not close friends at all. The quiet, the silence, has permitted an intimacy that I think we both enjoy. I want her to have a good life. I think she will make an outstanding advocate. Both her heart and her brain are focused on social justice. And because she is not a kid straight out of undergraduate school, I feel confident she will stay that way. We discuss our different views on law school and other topics. Law school is a lot of work. It consumes you, if you are lucky.

Water aerobics is at 11:30 today. It will be hard to get a nicer day than yesterday when the sky was blue, undisturbed by a single cloud or contrail. The thermometer said 78 impossible degrees. This is February! It is too early to tell what today might bring, but the doors to the porch are standing ajar for our venturesome cat, and the air feels soft.

Next to last planned activity of the day is a book club meeting. Upper Case, not the Whatevers. But like the Whatevers, we read what we want and talk to one another about our personal readings.

My sister-in-law is a big reader and has a huge soft spot for mysteries, especially mystery series. But if I find something I have loved, even if it isn't a mystery, she reads it, and we can talk about it. My offerings this month will be *Machines Like Me* by Ian McEwan; *100 Years of the Greatest Short Stories*, edited by Lorrie Moore; and *Garden of Marvels* by Ruth Kassinger. I am still reading the last two, but that is fine. This isn't a race or competition. And I am just delighted to be back among the readers of the world. For a few months I was afraid I'd never read anything again. Unsupportable. Whew.

My bridge friends are doing another four-way call at 3:30 this afternoon because ML is in rehab after an infection in her leg suddenly laid her low. We need to hear her voice, hear straight from her how she is doing. When is she going to be released from rehab hell? So many questions. How does one get an infection in her leg?

Friday night. I am going to make something easy for supper, and Kent and I will stretch out in our matching chairs and watch *Jeopardy*, catch up on the series we are enjoying. We are safe. Vaccinated and tucked into our Hobbit Hole. The people we love are safe. My life is embarrassingly good.

From Hutchinson to Yokohama

The Navy, in all its wisdom, decided to move us from Hutchinson, Kansas, to Yokohama, Japan. It was 1955, just ten years after the end of World War II, and the "us" was my Navy pilot father, my adaptable mom, and me, aged ten, Larry aged eight, and Marty, aged two. "Us" also included our beloved cocker spaniel, Tippy, because we all loved the dog, and dammit, the dog was going to Japan with us. It was not quite like our previous ten moves. For one thing, my parents usually mapped the straightest route from one post to the next. Driving with three kids and a dog will do that for you. But this time, my well-meaning parents decided to see our country's beautiful Western side. We would drive to San Francisco where we would board a MSTS ship. [Military Sea Transport Service.]

There was no interstate in those days. Signs were posted, "Last opportunity for gas for the next 250 miles". Cars were not air conditioned, and radio beacons were short and timid in the wide-open spaces. When I think of it now, the I-have-to-tinkles, the where-are-wes, the I'm-hungrys, the Mom-Larry-touched-mes, it is a wonder that our parents did not just leave us by the side of the road.

They had plans. The Royal Gorge, the Painted Desert, The Grand Canyon, The Monuments of the Gods, The Petrified Forest. But the Painted Desert, for example, is layers of rock in subtle desert colors. Beautiful and amazing to adults, not as good as Larry's comic book. He refused to get out of the car. "I don't want to look at dirt."

Dad said Larry acted like this because he was clearly Mom's son, while Mom said Larry was his Dad's son, right to the marrow. Marty and I at least got out of the car. Of the three of us, I probably have the most intact memories. Larry was deep in his comic books, and Marty was only two. When I see our home movies, details come back to me. The Grand Canyon was amazing, and Mother said about fifty times not to get too close to the edge. We climbed Pike's Peak, and there was snow in June.

What I really, really remember about that trip was a trip my dad and I took to get something from a drug store in San Francisco. We came around a corner, and there was a huge, huge man with pink hair to his shoulders. This was 1955, people. I literally gasped. "Paula Sue," said my dad in a stage whisper. "Get over here." He looked into my startled face and said very quietly, "That is Gorgeous George. He's a professional wrestler."

Okay, okay, The Painted Desert and Monuments of the Gods were fine. But GORGEOUS GEORGE! An enormous man with shoulder length pink hair. I could barely keep myself inside my skin, I was so excited. I couldn't wait to tell Larry.

We went to Japan on the *Gaffey* and returned on the *Patrick*. The ships were named for generals. They were both painted Navy-ship gray and were functional for moving military men and their dependents. And their dogs. The bad part was that poor Tippy had to endure in a cage when we are arrived in Japan. He had a six-week quarantine.

The *Gaffey* and the *Patrick* were not cruise ships. None of us had ever been on a cruise ship, in any case, and I loved being on the sea. I had seen the Atlantic, the Gulf of Mexico, but nothing prepared me for the uncontained power of the Pacific Ocean. I could, and did, sit for hours watching that huge sea thrash and boil near the wake of our ship. The beautiful color and the clear danger were right there to be seen. No camouflage, no beach full of people laughing and playing at its edge to soften the effect, nothing but a simple railing to separate me from a force I had never imagined. Ferocity and beauty.

I had broken my wrist before we left Hutchinson, and it was time for the cast to come off. My dad told this story over and over because he claimed it was a perfect illustration of who I was. Hutchinson had these unusually tall curbs, supposedly to keep the tumble weed in the streets. It was the custom of the children to ride their bikes straight at these curbs and jump them. We did it all the time. No biggie.

One day just before we left, I aimed my bicycle at a curb, screwed up the timing, and slammed into the curb and flew over the handle bars. I did not hurt myself. I could have just lifted the bike to the sidewalk from there, but instead, I backed the bike up and charged the curb again. This time, when I flew over the handlebars, I broke my wrist. You say stubborn, I say undaunted. Potayto, potahto.

Mom located a corpsman on the *Gaffey* who had never removed a cast but grabbed my arm with cavalier indifference and started sawing through the cast. "Let me know if I cut you," he grinned. On the way out of the infirmary, the ship hit a swell, and I slammed that arm against the bulkhead to steady myself. Didn't hurt much at all.

The *Gaffey* pulled into Yokohama after we stopped for a day or two in Hawaii. This was not the land of Panasonic and Sony. It was right out of a dream about Japan. Men dressed in a sort of breechcloth and wearing a reed cape around their shoulders moved boxes and containers all over the wharf.

This was the start of the most exotic adventure. This was better than looking at dirt, better than comics, better than long, pink hair. This was a world we could hardly imagine. We were going to live here. We were so excited that, for once, my noisy family hushed and took in the deep green, the beauty, the excitement of Japan. We were home. It had never looked like this before. And I know now, it never would again.

FSU, Florida State University

If you went to Florida State in the early sixties, something amazing happened. You entered one school and era and emerged four years later from an entirely different school and era.

When I first arrived in Tallahassee in 1963, I felt I had climbed into the way-back machine and found myself in the early fifties. We still had the same rules that had governed the women attending FSCW, Florida State College for Women. And FSCW, a women's college, had become coed and emerged from its pupa in 1949.

Janie, one of the Roomies, had two sons. They asked her repeatedly to tell them about all the drugs that everyone was doing. I mean we went to college in the 60's, right? LSD? Timothy Leary? Marijuana? But the disappointing, absolutely true facts are that not only did we not do drugs, but we did not know anyone who did.

Oh, there was a lot of drinking that went on. Including grain alcohol. We were our own kind of stupid. Long before the Ichetucknee became a state park, we would load up two cars with inner tubes, fried chicken from Tucker's Restaurant, and something called Purple Jesus. It was grain alcohol and Welch's grape juice. We poured this over a large block of ice in a metal washtub that we then put in the middle of its own inner tube. We telescoped straws together to make them very long and floated down the Ichetucknee with the Purple Jesus floating in the middle of us, sipping from our expanded straws. That any of us lived to adulthood is amazing.

In '63 I wore panty hose, skirts to my knee. In about '65, we had no skirt longer than midthigh. Miniskirts and minidresses with patterned or opaque pantyhose were in. In November of 1963, President Kennedy was killed, and we went to his memorial service in Westcott in hats and gloves. My God, what a heart-breaking time. Then we watched the Beatles on the only television screen in the dorm, downstairs in the basement. Nothing was ever the same. We wanted to dress like the Brits. Carnaby Street? Gone were the Ladybug dresses with their tucked bodices and Peter Pan collars. In came vivid colors, crazy prints, and paper dresses. (Yes, I had a couple of paper dresses and in Tallahassee... the main issue was not to get caught in the rain wearing one.)

In 1963 there were hootenannies. In 1965, it was Eve of Destruction. By 1967, 1963 was a generation away. And I bought my clothes at the Army/Navy Surplus Store.

But the main worry was the draft. Vietnam loomed huge in everyone's brain. It was on our television news every night. It was our boyfriends, our brothers, dying for something no one quite understood. There were protests, assassinations of Martin Luther King, Malcom X, and the Kennedy brothers. We were scared, enraged, motivated, but what we were not is high. Sorry, guys. We really didn't do that.

The Gardening Gene

Both of my parents were gardeners. They loved gardens, planted gardens, happily maintained them, and were heard to rush into the house to exclaim when a new shoot appeared, a bud opened. So, my own love of dirt, pots and plants did not really come as a surprise, although neither of my brothers showed the slightest interest. Daisies? Roses? Whatever.

The thing about my parents' gardening was that they rented our various houses. They moved into some barely inhabitable rental and immediately got to work making it livable. They always planted a garden. I remember that when we lived in Brunswick, Georgia, Mom got into gladiolas. She planted a huge swathe of them. They were glorious. In VA, it was roses, especially a very pale lavender rose called Sterling Silver. It was lovely. In MD, it was peonies, but the Japanese beetles were just deadly, and I think Mom lost that battle. In NJ, Mom planted heavenly blue morning glories, and I fell in love with flowers.

When I was very little, maybe about five, Mom planted a vegetable garden behind the house. I was mesmerized. You put in these tiny seeds, and carrots and radishes came up! Amazing. A kind of magic really. Mom's main challenge was getting me to leave the plants in the ground long enough for them to mature. I wanted to check on their metamorphosis. And when one was allowed to grow long enough, we picked it together, washed it off, and had a feast. Oh, how I love those memories.

But the veggie gardens were not usual. Flowers is what it was all about. We both were, I still am, just gaga over flowers. The wonder of their many shapes and the brightness of their colors. I have been a gardener my entire adult life, and it has always been flowers.

I did not marry an itinerant military man, and Harry and I lived in the same house for the thirty-two years of our marriage, and I continued to live there for another nine years after his death. You can do a lot of gardening in forty-one years. He had bought a house with a big lawn and a few foundation plantings. It had lots of pine trees and a chain-link fence.

By the time I left that property, I had built a series of patios in the front and in the back. I had disappeared the chain-link fence behind azaleas. I set myself the task of planting three azaleas a week until I had covered the whole area. I built a long arbor with plantings of kiwi vine [an annual sacrifice to the squirrels], and a large pergola planted with wisteria over the largest patio. Harry adored dogwood trees, and we planted about a dozen of them. And I planted a Japanese maple that just glows brilliant red in the fall.

Every winter, I would dream about what new things I would plant in the garden. I read gardening books and learned the hard way that plants that are "full sun" in New England, are NOT "full sun" here. We were proud of our hard work and took enormous pleasure as it emerged, changed course.

I made some dreadful mistakes. I planted moso bamboo after seeing it in Japan. It was like some demented force in the garden, sending up knee high bamboo shoots overnight right outside a window. I swear it was stalking me. No pun intended. Harry told me he wanted his ashes scattered in that garden. They are.

The house has changed hands a couple of times since I sold it. Of course, everyone who buys a home wants to make it theirs. The latest buyers brought in a tractor to dig everything up.

Gone are the camellias, the ivy, forty-one years of effort. They had turf laid everywhere. It has come full circle. We had friends marry in that yard; our number two son had an engagement party there. We laughed and sang on those patios every year after our Passover Seder.

All those good memories of happy times, of family watershed moments, form a kind of aura around the house when I look at it now. It is colored by nostalgia. I hope the people who live there now love that garden as we did. In their own distinctive way.

Gerry

Geraldine Blumburg Levitt was my mother. She hated her name, and everyone called her Gerry. Well, except children and grandchildren, nieces, nephews. Not those who were supposed to call her by their relationship to her and not her name. Isn't it strange that we do that?

She was born July 10, 1925, and this would have been her 96th birthday had she not died in September of 2003. She had lustrous black hair, brown eyes and was, by her definition, tall. To everyone else's definition, she was five foot five.

She had a laugh that could be heard around the neighborhood. She was opinionated, smart, loved words and languages, cooking, music, gardening, knitting and, above all other things on this earth, she loved our father, Ben Bernard Levitt. They had met when they were about twelve and thirteen in Miami when their families were attending the same wedding.

I do not know of a greater gift that parents can give their children than to be in love with one another. Mom would be working in the kitchen, and Dad would walk up from behind her, put his arms around her waist and kiss the side of her head. They were nineteen and twenty-one when they married. Children, really.

My mom and I had a love/hate relationship that had never been resolved when she died. The hate part did not happen until after I went to college. My mother said about me, "I sent her to college a pussycat, and she came home a saber tooth tiger." We shared many loves which my mom said was an indication I was competing with her. I too love cooking, words and languages, gardening. We loved much of the same music.

Many people in my life have said I am competing with them. If I am, I am not aware of it. But I will admit that, if I do anything, I do it the very best I can. I learned almost everything I do well from my mother.

My mom never ever said to any of her children or grandchildren that they should be like her. She wanted us to emulate Dad. He was handsome, smart, canny, had enormous integrity, made friends easily, fair, you name it. And he was a great man. But he would not have been nearly as successful as he was without her total support, her total Team Levitt all-in spirit.

The woman moved three children and a cocker spaniel approximately thirty times before my dad retired from the Navy. Thirty times, she made some strange house, Quonset hut, into a home. Thirty times. While schlepping three kids.

When he started his own company, Mom came to work for the company as his most trusted and valued employee. She was his security officer. There was nothing she would not do for him, but that was not always reciprocated.

Right after he retired from the Navy, my father worked for the Cornell Aeronautical Labs near Buffalo, New York. I won't even start on the lack of pizzazz that is Buffalo's curse. I put it right after Hutchinson, Kansas in my pantheon of dreadful places we had to live.

Finally, all my siblings were in college, out of the house, or old enough not to need a fulltime cook and bottlewasher. Mom got an idea to make flower topiaries for bathrooms that had a small vial of perfume hidden in the arrangement. She had a wonderful eye and bought the most gorgeous silk flowers.

Each topiary was in its own flowerpot and wrapped in clear cellophane that had Mom's name on it: Boutique Geri. They sold like hotcakes. Holy Moly. She could barely keep up with her orders. The company was Dad and her. Period. Dad painted the flowerpots and probably kept the books. Mom shopped for the flowers and other materials, perfumes, made contact with various sellers, and delivered the product.

For the first time in her life, she had money in her account that she had earned herself. She did not have to ask Dad for money to buy him a gift. She could do it herself! She was so proud. She bought him a gorgeous, very expensive watch, and beyond question, the giver was at least as pleased as the receiver.

Dad decided to leave Cornell Labs and start his own operations research company. He took classes from the Wharton School and finally said to Mom, "Let's do this." And they moved one more time.

This time they moved to Maryland because it is close to D.C. and its research needs. But Dad said, "I can't do Boutique Geri with you anymore. You can do it on your own." My mom begged. But Dad felt he had to give his full attention to the new company. Mom let Boutique Geri die, turning down orders, and not contacting new sellers. I think it broke her heart.

My parents are buried in Maryland where none of us lives. Not even close. They, of course, are buried together. It was a day in early October when she was buried, and a tree just a few yards from her grave site was sending out hundreds of seeds on each gust of wind. The sun shone, the tree tossed seeds of life and renewal into the air. And, I thought, Mom.

Covid Chronicles 9: 6/28/20

How to distract yourself when you have read, written, cooked, eaten, and gardened your way through the last five months and are now in some mental nowhere land where neurons only occasionally bump against one another in what was once a functioning brain. I cannot suggest listening to the news. I have cut way, way back on listening or reading the news since the pandemic arrived because my anxiety went to heights never previously documented. I apparently hit overload if I try to process politics and pandemic simultaneously. And every time they coalesce, as in afternoon briefings by POTUS and the Servile Dwarves, I swear with a breadth and depth of scatological phrases I had apparently been saving up in some obscure corner of my mind for just the right moment. It has arrived, and the ghost of my mother is horrified.

Today started me on a rant that led to this note. Trump has decided to ignore the ruling the Supreme Court recently announced on the DACA Dreamers. He is going to do what he wants to do. He has simultaneously installed his own troops in twenty-five Democratic cities throughout our country. "Because the local police there won't do the right thing," he says.

Are you still reading this? Why aren't we all standing outside, screaming at the top of our lungs? If Paul Revere were alive, who would he tell about this domestic invasion? Where are our senators? Comatose? Congress? Democratic leadership? Republican leadership? Chief Justice Roberts? The Head of the

Joint Chiefs of Staff? Anyone? Hello? Any American leaders still alive out there? Is this pandemic so over-whelming that we cannot defend our country simultaneously?

What treason can he induce that will be so awful that our country is dragged from its sleep? Our country, our three-equal-branches-of-government democracy, will be tear-gassed and truncheoned while people take to the streets to protest wearing masks. Dear God. Please, please, please. I am so scared. I have a pandemic outside my door and a virus in the White House. I keep reminding myself of all that we have endured as a nation. Assassinations, police riots, elections questioned, wars inside and out, civil unrest, racism are all part of our history. And we endured. But this may be the lethal combination. Without opposition, without leaders, how can we resist?

Mr. Trump has a plan for this country. Do we have a counterplan? Hello? Anyone?

Leap Year, 2020

My Go-Take-a-Flying-Leap List:

1. Donald Trump. Usually, I can find one redeeming characteristic in a person that at least moderates my dislike. Donald Trump is an exception to that rule. He is a boor and a thug. That the Republicans chose him out of seventeen candidates to represent their party is simply staggering. Which brings me to number two on my list.

2. Republicans. What happened to you? What happened to the party of Eisenhower, Reagan, McCain? A national debt in excess of a trillion dollars? Should we all be looking for pods in our basements? How can you face your grandchildren after ignoring climate change? How can you face yourselves in the mirror after allowing children to be torn from their parents and put in camps?

3. Democrats. Here's an idea: work together instead of eviscerating one another. Together. Unity. I was impressed by the intelligence, experience and ideas at your debates, until you started snarling and tearing one another apart. Let me explain this as simply as possible: I am now a one issue voter, something I swore I would never, ever be. But here I am. Any one of you, from Bernie to Amy and everyone in between. I want to know one thing: can you beat Donald Trump. If not, get the hell out

of the way and support the person who can. STOP being hatchet men for the Republicans. They can do that all by themselves.

4. James Comey. Dante saved a circle in hell just for this man. But for James Comey and his absurd and ill-advised decision to troll out Hillary's emails the week before the election, we would have a President fluent in the English language. Want to know why all the prognosticators were saying Hillary was going to win? Because they were relying on data that came out before James Comey felt it necessary to wander into the elections process so close to election day that they had no time to take the country's temperature after it caught the email flu. Comey elected Trump. That Trump then fired him is the kind of poetic justice I love. But we are still stuck with Trump.

5. The NRA. What can I possibly say that has not been said before? People have been gunned down in the one place supposed to be a sanctuary for all: our churches, synagogues, mosques. Elementary school children, high school kids, people enjoying a concert or going to a movie, people at work, people on military bases. People answering calls for help, people shopping. Random people. Women doing yoga. Life has no order or meaning. Random shots and random people killed. Don't give me that Second Amendment crap; I wasn't born yesterday. How about that Third Amendment? Does that one still resonate with you too? You have decided that selling guns is more important than people's lives! You are the scum on capitalism's shoe.

Okay. I am happy to note that I had more than twice as many things to be thankful for at Thanksgiving than I have to fume about.

Mother's Day I

It is Mother's Day! As if a single day were enough to hold all the thanks, the tears, the laughter and love, the pain of being a mother. As if.

My own mother was a larger-than-life individual who was creative to such an extent that she made her own universe, her own reality. Nothing as simplistic and fundamental as facts could stand in her way. This was confusing for a young girl who could not understand that reality was not good enough for Mom. An embroidered, hyperbolic, expanded life was what she wanted. So, she made one.

For me, this meant that if my mother told us something, how their parents had come to live in America, for example, I would look to Dad for confirmation. "Is this true, Dad?"

And he would often look askance and say, "Something like that."

It is only as an adult with documents shared among my cousins that I have seen the still amazing but more prosaic truth. Sometimes on a family Zoom, I launch into a story, only to have one or another say, "No, it did not happen like that."

I appreciate the truth. I do not find her to be the ugliest of the story-telling sisters at all. I admire her simple elegance. Mom never understood that in rejecting the truth of who we were by inventing people who were taller, smarter, prettier, more accomplished, that she rejected us. *Rejected her children.* We were ordinary people who had their successes and their near misses.

One of our all-out successes was the celebration of Mother's Day when we were children. This inevitably involved breakfast in bed and some absurd tchotchke we had purchased with a dollar contributed from Dad. The breakfast arrived too early at the bedside and sloshed all over a tray. It was cold cereal or nothing. We may have found a flower from the yard to make the tray more celebratory. The tray was quickly put aside, and Larry and I invited into the big bed with Mom and Dad, and the sudden tickle attacks and snuggles made the day.

Sometimes we would all pile into the family Buick for an aimless ride, sometimes stopping for ice cream, just moving through the countryside while Mom sang, and we stared at the ordinary world outside the windows as yet sadly unadorned and unpainted by Mom's imagination. "Can you imagine," she says, as she swivels around in her seat to face us, "how this place must have looked when the Indians lived here? What would that have been like?"

And off we would go. Out the car windows, into the trees, back a few centuries to another place and time.

Happy Mother's Day, Mom.

Obituary for Myself

I have written my obituary. There is nothing surprising about this if you know me: total control freak who likes to have the last word. It is in a notebook I keep at the desk so that, at my death, people know where everything is located.

My obituary is not even a little bit sad or morbid. But I also didn't want one of those obituaries that sound like I am applying for a job in the afterlife. Attended, was awarded, blah, blah, blah. Part of that obituary says how happy I am to have been born in America, especially if I was tagged to be a woman and a Jew. This country, balky and illogical as it can be, has made it possible for me to have the good life I have enjoyed.

My grandparents came here to escape Russia in the early twentieth century. The tale of their escape, which is hair-raising, my dad's position as the first in his family born in this country and the patriotism and gratitude of my family have formed me. Many, many times over the last four years, I have thought of tearing the whole thing up and starting over. I am exhausted by the malfeasance and misfeasance I have witnessed in government in the last four years. I have cried in frustration and at the villainy.

But now I think, *Wait.* Life is not over, and our country is not over. We still have a tale to tell. It will be like the Queen Mary on high seas, but we can change course. We can turn things around. I don't know if I will live to see it.

I am not ill with anything except being mortal. I am seventy-five, and my mother died at eighty. Time's winged chariot has turned into a Harley, roaring in my ear. On the news, we are informed that the pandemic will not go away and life will not return to normal just because we get vaccinated. Ever naïve, I had hoped that that was exactly what would happen. My messenger DNA would do its job, and I would take off my mask and throw open my front door, hug everyone I know, and have a huge party. Maybe not. And so long as every facet of government must be focused first on the physical and mental health of its citizens, I am afraid not much headway will be made on this course correction thing. There is a whole world to make well.

And so, I wonder if this is what the end of my life will be like. Will we continue, post-vaccination, to self-isolate? Will we be in our hobbit holes for the rest of my life? Will I never again attend a symphony or my grandsons' birthdays?

I'm glad I wrote that obituary when I did. But I am not quite ready to exit stage left; I want to see what the next four years will bring.

Orchids on Rosa

Awhile back, I wrote a confessional about how I had abandoned my orchids to the freeze of a night that snuck up on me. I was devastated. Many of my orchids are gifts from people I love and are named things like the Selby Orchid, the Josephine Orchid. Every day, I catalog new growth, the loss of a leaf, blooms, I look for spider mites [curse you!], and general malaise. I always watch my YouTube tutorials on orchids on their porch so we can all be on the same page, so to speak.

This is an update on the survivors and a valedictory to the resilience of life in general.

After the freeze, I lovingly took each pot, one by one [I have about seventy] and carefully examined it. Orchids don't show the effects of poor care immediately. These were full of tightly furled buds, racemes just emerging, shiny new leaves. But as I continued my close examination, a bud would fall, a leaf would begin to wither. And slowly, the sad effects of my neglect began to emerge. I could have kicked myself around the block for every single blossom I lost. Drat and double drat.

The Josephine orchid who lords it over the lesser orchids in her big maroon pot went from twelve leaves to one leaf. One. Josephine gave me that orchid on my 70th birthday, so she was huge. One of the minion orchids lost every single leaf, all buds. She was nothing but a single green leafless stem arising from her pot. The Selby orchid shed leaves, buds; I could have cried. But I watered them.

We listened together to a YouTube on what to do if you mess up badly and freeze your orchids. And something miraculous happened. Life happened. And it is a miracle every time you see it push back the odds and emerge with new growth, new blooms, new vigor. Yup, there was nothing but burial for two or three. Resuscitation is well above my pay grade. But I am taking a page from my sports-loving husband: it is a rebuilding year.

The Selby orchid has sixteen soft pink blooms open. The Josephine orchid has about five bright green new leaves; and the minion orchid has two bright, shiny leaves emerging. In spite of my gross negligence, life pushed back.

Most of the babies came from various grocery stores. They are bred to survive the drowning of eager stock boys and the full sun of negligent managers. They were bred to be tough, and bless their little hearts, I may have a collection of ninja orchids.

I think tough and beautiful may be one of my favorite combinations. And smart.

Winter: Visiting Dad

My father, Ben Levitt, died when he was 86 years old. He would say, if he were still here, that he only felt 85. He lived in Gaithersburg, Maryland. At the time he was dying, his two remaining children lived in Florida and Pennsylvania.

My younger brother, Marty, was the Librarian for the American Philosophical Society and a professor at Temple University. I was a lawyer. We were both deeply focused on our work. Our mother had died five years earlier. There were no neighbors, no family, no matter how distant, to keep Dad in that house in Gaithersburg. But he refused to move.

Both Marty and I literally begged him to come live with one of us or live in a facility closer to one of us. Not a chance. Dad's statement that stopped all conversation was that he felt closer to our mother in that house. They were married for sixty years. Marty's take on all this was that the convenience of his children is the last thing on his mind.

Marty is not an unrepentant hard ass; a fact is a fact. Dad has been stubborn all his life, and he and our mother, in direct opposition to the current trend, expected their children to live with whatever decision they made. Period. It was their life.

My father did not waiver with the passage of time. Sadly, the passage of time changed him in other ways that were exacerbated by this unwavering self-determination. He had a rare neurological disease called Multiple Systems Atrophy.

This is what happens: unlike Alzheimer's disease which attacks the cognitive parts of the brain, MSA hits the autonomic nervous system *and* the cognitive areas. His brain is forgetting how to regulate his blood pressure, how to swallow, how to apprehend the words that he can no longer read. He is forgetting how to walk, how to use his hands, how to control his elimination. When my father could still joke, he called it Multiple Systems Entropy. It is terminal. There was no protocol for this disease when he died in 2008.

Sometimes, I have to wonder what is the worse outcome: to be trapped, cogent, inside a body with all physical functions run amuck and unresponsive to your needs, or to be trapped in that same non-firing machine of a body but unaware of what is happening.

I watched *Awakenings* recently. People were frozen in catatonic states after surviving encephalitis. One psychiatrist asks another if these frozen people are aware of what has happened to them. The doctor answers in the negative. The first psychiatrist asks how he knows? And his colleague answers, "Because anything else would be unthinkable."

It is thinkable. I think about it all the time.

Dad was born in 1923 in Miami, Florida. His parents and older siblings had left Russia through the frigid Eastern door of Harbin, China. There was an entire community of Russian Jews who had escaped Russia and had formed a community in Harbin. They lived there for a few years, then lived in Japan for a few years before they finally settled in Miami.

My dad and his younger brother were the first family members to be born in the U.S. The "Amerikaners", his parents and sibs would tease. His father wanted Dad to be a physician. Medicine carries across international borders. People are people. Their biology is the same in South America as in

Australia or Europe. Jews have to move a lot unexpectedly. Law, for example, does not travel well. Businesses with any kind of inventory do not travel well. But medicine travels. Ben should be a doctor. Dad, ever master of his fate, had other ideas.

A blimp had landed at Homestead Airbase when he was about nine years old. Dad rode his bicycle for miles in the Florida sun to see this goliath up close. The blimp crew was giving people an opportunity to see inside the gondola or basket that cleaves to the underside of the huge bag, holding the crew and the controls. Dad waited in line. Finally, he was there, front of the line. One of the crew was delighted to see a young kid there and showed him all around, taking special time with him, letting him try the controls. That did it. Blimps.

Dad got to blimps by going to the Naval Academy. When he graduated, five of his class volunteered for Lighter Than Air Duty. Dad spent World War II in blimps, convoying ships from Europe to Africa.

His father died when Dad was a plebe at the Academy. He must have known by then that his son, Ben, was not going to be a doctor. I have no idea if he knew Dad was going to become John Wayne.

Dad's sense of himself is apparent from his earliest life. Jewish boys do not grow up to pilot blimps. Jewish boys of Russian immigrant parents are not likely candidates for any military academies. Many Jews fled Europe to avoid induction in the Czar's army, a fate that was surely a death sentence. Indeed, with the possible exception of some biblical heroes, Jews did not have much of a pro-military persona until after 1947 when the State of Israel emerged and announced, "Never Again" and proceeded to put some muscle behind those words. Dad was already a blimp pilot by then. When the blimps were ultimately retired, Dad became a jet pilot.

The Navy decided where we would live. There may or may not have been a single other Jew in town. There certainly were no other Jewish jet pilots in Hutchinson, Kansas; Yokohama, Japan; or even in Toms River, New Jersey, to name a few of his postings. He was simply out there by himself, being Ben. Being the man he chose to be. Inventing himself.

His partner in crime in this endeavor was my mother, Gerry Levitt. They had met as children and married when my mother was two weeks past her nineteenth birthday. Dad was twenty-one and just out of the academy. There was a war on.

My mother thought that my father was the smartest, handsomest, most amazing man in the world. She was his staunchest ally, his best PR man. I know this because she told us so repeatedly.

In their later years, they sometimes sounded like squabbling children, but God help the child who got crossways with either of them. There would be no quarter offered by the other parent. If Dad said they were moving to Japan just ten years after the conclusion of the war, Mother would say, "Shall I pack mosquito netting?"

My dad was an athlete. He was about 6 feet 3 inches tall and had a natural grace and ease in his body. He was an excellent golfer, bowler, and handball player. He exercised daily, long before people were jogging, joining health clubs, working on specific muscle groups or worrying about their cardio rates. He played killer handball into his late 70's. He was never overweight, took pride in doing all things well and all things in moderation. He attempted to pilot a high-altitude balloon across the country, crashing in the Mexican desert. He won an award for flight endurance in a blimp. After he retired from the Navy, he started his own operations research company that grew to have offices in Maine, California, Italy and Hawaii. He was successful in almost everything he chose to take on.

In true 50's fashion, Dad was more of a family icon than a father. He was deferred to when home, but he was seldom home. He worked outside the home. It was for Mother to do the work inside the home, including rearing the children. My dad attended my high school graduation. Period. He did not attend a single parent conference, induction ceremony, play or concert we were in. He once told me that if he had to do it all again, he would not have had children.

He invented himself out of whole cloth. Through sheer force of will, he created Ben Levitt. He was not about to concede any of that control and independence to the boring disabilities of age or illness. He was furious that his body had betrayed him. He maintained it, never abused it, was never seriously ill in his life. How could it so completely fail him now? And why couldn't the doctors stop the advance of the illness, the advance of age? He fought every inevitability that his circumstances required. I think he really believed he was entitled to an exemption from the travails of old age.

So, Marty was right. Dad was not about to make his care more convenient for his children. Dug into his home in Maryland, surrounded by the detritus of a family that had either died or moved away, he had a taproot that seemed to run to China. Once a month, I took a Friday off and flew to Gaithersburg, Maryland from Tallahassee, Florida. It was expensive, exhausting, frustrating and depressing. I estimate I did this sixty times. It is also the only time in my life that I had a chance to have a one-on-one relationship with the exasperating and exceptional man who was my father. I knew there wasn't much time left.

Whenever I came through that last set of doors at Dulles Airport, the doors separating the arriving travelers from their waiting families and friends, I scanned the area for my parents. In my mind's eye, I could still see them as they used to be, waiting for me. My mother had been dead for years, my father incapable of the long ride from his home to the airport, but still, I looked for them.

I headed straight for the taxi stand, and a man from Afghanistan, Pakistan, sometimes Iran or India, took me from Dulles to my parents' home. It was a long ride. At least 40 minutes with the traffic moving. If the plane was late arriving, or the only available flight was later in the day, we could be stuck in gridlock traffic on the Beltway for hours. To avoid this, I rose at 4:30 in the morning to catch a 6 or 7 AM flight. If all went moderately well, I would be at Dad's home by 1:30 that afternoon. The other reason for this absurdly early flight is the cost of the airline tickets. If you were willing to fly at 6 in the morning, to get to the airport by 4 as security now demands, to rise by 3 to make the trip to the airport in a timely fashion, you can save $150 or more on an economy class ticket. The trip to the airport in Tallahassee is only about 20 minutes that early in the morning. But in the D.C. area, there is surprising traffic. I had to allow for the unexpected.

When the cab pulled into Dad's suburban driveway, Rosa, my parents' longtime housekeeper and caretaker, greeted me with a warm hug. "Ah, Mrs. Pawlah!" She was maybe as much as five feet tall, a native of Nicaragua. Her English was better than my Spanish, but we used both languages to make ourselves understood. She came to work for my parents about twenty-five years earlier. They grew very fond of one another. She helped daily when my mother was dying and promised my mother that she would look out for my father.

He needed looking after. He could not make his mandatory pot of coffee for himself, could not dress himself. Even though there was a motorized chair lift on the stairway, he could not get from the top floor of the house to the floor with the kitchen, living room and dining room. He could not get onto the lift chair or off of it on his own. And ultimately, he forgot how to push the button that makes it move along its track.

The house was in need of basic maintenance. My mother must be spinning in her grave. The outside of the house needed paint and cleaning. My mother's once beautiful garden was struggling. The plants around the patio were all dead. In the front, some money-hungry yard-man had massacred my mother's most precious tree, a glorious Kwanzan cherry that bloomed right outside the big bay window by the kitchen table. Its graceful limbs reached nearly to the roof of this two-story house, and each spring, it was a pink cloud of double blossoms. The entire family loved it. It was the highway of choice for the squirrels, refuge for the birds, and hiding place for the chipmunks at its roots. It brought tears to my eyes to see such beloved beauty needlessly and thoughtlessly destroyed. Someone broke the lock to the shed in the backyard in which my parents stored all their gardening tools. The door stood ajar. They were robbed, but no one had even bothered to see what was taken. No one remembered exactly what was in there.

Inside, Rosa had struggled to maintain some sense of order and cleanliness in the midst of rotating shifts of nurses' aides, strangers moving through the house with callous disregard of what may be precious to the people who lived there. The chairs in the dining room had begun to break, perhaps just the glue failing after many years of use. But I also walked into our dining room once to find an aide leaned back in a dining room chair, her feet planted firmly on my mother's beloved dining room table. She ignored me.

The chairs in the kitchen area were a motley collection of chairs brought from other areas of the house as the kitchen chairs, too, began to break. No one attempted to fix them. They were left leaning at sad angles against the dining room wall. There were streaks of dirt or some melted fixative weeping down the walls in the living room behind the pictures there. The green paint was dirty. Dad's sometimes needed wheelchair was folded into one corner. The green wall to wall carpet was stained and nasty looking, although Rosa had it professionally cleaned and attempted everything she could think of to remove the stains.

The bathrooms were the worst. Staying there was like staying at a cheap motel. Toilets broke down, the hot water heater had to be replaced, the bathrooms flooded, they needed all new paint, complete refurbishing. The tile had lifted in my dad's bathroom.

In his favorite haunt, the family room, his chair, a huge recliner, listed on its base. It had to be kicked smartly to get the footrest to stay down. My mother's mechanical chair that lifted her to a standing position and eased her down again was sticky and barely moved. The television set was topped with stuffed animals, survivors of long-ago gift baskets. On the shelves were the Lladro and other collectibles from a sixty-year marriage. Their perfectly painted porcelain eyes watched the encroaching chaos with cool detachment.

The house, like my father, was dying. One was dying from lack of maintenance, the other in spite of maintenance. There is a lesson there.

My father was a mere husk of the man he had been. Age and compressing vertebrae had reduced him to less than six feet. He was so thin that when I saw him sleeping, saw his bony face and open mouth, he looked like a cadaver. His skin was bruised, purple and torn from falling against walls and bumping into things. He had complete upper and lower dentures which he wore, irregularly, but not affixed to his gums in any way. He had had them adjusted and fine-tuned several times, but they still hurt his mouth. When he fell asleep in his cantankerous chair, his dentures would fall out of his mouth and sit pink and grotesque on his chest. He drooled and could not feel the saliva escaping his mouth. He was aware of what had happened to him, how he looked, and there were few people he would allow to visit.

In the hottest weather, he wore a cardigan sweater over a flannel shirt over an undershirt. He was constantly cold. Still, he refused to adopt the jogging suit/sweat suit uniform of the elderly. His shirts had collars, he wore a belt on his polyester slacks, socks and casual shoes, but not running shoes or sneakers. He had his standards for matching pants, shirt and sweater. He had blue days and brown days.

He shaved, to greater and lesser effect each day. Or someone shaved him and brushed his thin, white hair. Someone. One of the many aides cycling through the revolving door of his needs. He would not let me help him dress or go to the bathroom, although he needed help with both. I may have been sixty-three years old, but I was still his daughter; he was still my father. A certain propriety, and pride, must be maintained.

When I walked into the kitchen from the carport, wrestling my carryon luggage into the house, he struggled to his feet to hug me close. He had been sitting by the window, waiting for me since he awoke that morning. "Susie Q," he said with a grin. We sat together at the kitchen table and over cups of coffee and a bagel for me, we reviewed my trip to Maryland in detail. What time I got up, was the plane crowded, did the plane leave and arrive on time, how was the ride, was there turbulence. If I was lucky enough to have an interesting travel companion seated next to me or I saw something unusual in the airport or plane, I stored this away to tell him. Once several soldiers in camouflage fatigues boarded the plane together. The passengers spontaneously burst into applause. I saw it happen at a gate once in North Carolina, too. Another time, I boarded a plane in Atlanta that was otherwise filled with Boy Scouts on the way to a national jamboree in Washington.

I described the taxi ride for him, told him about the driver, they were often bearded and exotically turbaned, the driver's country of origin, their families. I became a collector of the stories of how they came to live in the Washington, D.C. area, a collector of the portraits of the places they left behind, the pictures of the life they have made in the U.S. And he always asked how soon I had to go home. Sometimes, often, he reached across the table and held my hand while I chattered on. Sometimes, he fell asleep while I was talking. When he awoke, he said he had just been checking out the inside of his eyelids.

Usually, Dad was cogent. He always knew who I was. He was a bit confused on other members of the family, and so we frequently looked at old snapshots together. They were a wonderful jumping off place for free associating stories and for remembering how the family tree is spread. It was during one of these times that I learned about the blimp in Homestead, Florida, that he had visited as a boy.

Sometimes, I could help him remember details that he had forgotten. We both loved it when our combined memories were working to flesh out a time, an event, that was funny or dear to us both. Each of us was amazed at what the other remembered, at the randomness of what we have stored away and the randomness of what we have forgotten. What internal mechanism is deciding what we recall, what we forget.

I tried to bring photos of what is going on in my life now in Tallahassee. If there had been a party, if I had traveled, I brought the pictures to share. Short stories, collections of anecdotes, were great for reading aloud to Dad. He liked it but often fell asleep. I didn't care. Once he awakened, he'd say, "Where were we?" and I took up where we left off. I read novels to him, but my visits were so short that it was difficult to do something that long. *Marley & Me* was a success, and we both laughed at how I got teary at the sad parts.

One of our favorite things to do was for me to read the personals section of the paper to him. We hooted about the man who described himself as being in "navel" intelligence. People can be hilariously specific in what they are seeking. And some are so deeply pathetic. Other parts of the paper were also searched for good reading aloud and discussion topics. My father and I had never agreed politically, and I was careful about what I chose to read or discuss. I could tell he was being careful too. We were enjoying this time together, this connection. We did not want to disrupt it with disagreements. When I was a child, we had argued hotly on politics, religion, the right and wrong of so much in life. Now, we just wanted to be friends and companions. Let someone else man the battlements.

Dad was not blind, but he could no longer read. The advancing MSA made him aphasic to written language. So, he saved his magazines about Lighter-Than-Air, his pamphlets from his Academy class telling which classmate is where – or more often now who had died – for me to read to him. I learned more about high altitude balloons and blimps, their possible modern uses, the research ongoing in that field, than I ever even remotely wanted to know.

Finally, the last thing I could do for Dad when I visited was to cook for him. I remember the things he used to love, and I trot them out to please him. He had an amazingly good appetite and seemed to relish every bite. My mother loved to cook and was an accomplished baker, cook and experimenter in the kitchen. Many of our memories are bound up in the food we ate together, the holiday feasts Mom prepared, the occasional disaster, the daily meals and Sunday brunches.

The best times for visiting with Dad were when my brother and his wife visited at the same time I did. Then the house was full of Marty's laughter and humor, and I can see some semblance of the family we used to be. Dad engaged him in discussions about football and manly things. They had a special connection. Beth brought him wonderful treats, and I tried to cook something special. We realized, finally, that when we visited simultaneously, it wore Dad out. He would barely leave his bed for days after a joint visit. But that time was the gold in his life. And ours.

I realize that I have made a visit with my father seem like a whirlwind of activities. Not at all. Mostly what Dad did was sleep. For long hours, he slept in his chair in front of the television set. He could not stay awake. His body was exhausted from the stress of unregulated blood pressure and from the ravages of the MSA. When he was awake, we squeezed in whatever we could. I saw a lot of *Wheel of Fortune* and *Jeopardy* when I was there. But mostly, I sat and read my own book and watched Dad sleep. And sleep. And I looked around the house at all the ghosts of the people who had lived there, of the family we were, of the life that Ben Levitt created.

Dad died in his home, in my arms, June 23, 2008.

Southernmost

He calls himself "Southernmost." He's my cousin, David, and he lives in Key West. Based on the family we share in common, he probably has brown hair and eyes. But I wouldn't know him if he walked into the room. Neither of us can remember when we last met.

But when my husband had a stroke a couple of years ago, like a good gremlin, Southernmost reappeared in the mail. Tracing this through the family switchboard, I figure my father told his sister, who is David's mother, and that did it.

How to tell you about this mystery man? He sends funny cards and wildly unlikely "Care" packages – bags of Jelly Bellies, framed butterflies, children's stories, stuffed animals, gourmet tidbits, Key West cookbooks, magic tricks, books on tape and volumes of lawyer jokes.

When a niece or nephew starts college, David starts with the "Care" packages. His timing is uncanny. Exams getting to you? Lost a lover? Someone you love ill or hurt? Expect the unexpected.

Altruism is probably on the endangered concepts list. It is the very antithesis of *schadenfreude*. Do something to make someone else happy. Gain pleasure from another's laughter; expect no quid for your quo, no tit for your tat. A free lunch. I'll scratch your back, and you'll ... enjoy it.

He is the real thing. Oh sure, your family may have a Nobel Prize winner, an Olympic athlete, a lion of Wall Street among its number. We have "Southernmost." The ephemeral, fading, never-to-be-seen again altruist. Eat your heart out.

Thanksgiving 2020

There are so many wonderful things in my life that endure, no matter who is in power. I rant and rave about how the world could be a better place from a life of enormous privilege. I have shelter, food, and security. I have people I love and who reciprocate. I have had an education and a career; I have traveled around this world.

Here are more of the things for which I am grateful on this Pandemic-inflected Thanksgiving and every day of my lucky, lucky life:

1. My husband, Kent Putnam, who retired from lawyering, took up his camera, and began seeing and creating beauty everywhere he went. Our home showcases many of his works, and I am deeply proud of the man he has created at a time many simply take to their recliners and remote controls.

2. My brother and sister-in-law. Beth and Marty lived in the very heart of Philadelphia in a happy life so urban that they did not even own a car. When Marty retired and called me to say they were moving to Tallahassee, I flat out disbelieved him. I am so glad he surprised me. The last five years with them have just been wonderful. They are two very bright, well-read, creative people, full of piss and vinegar. We get together once a week, and I look forward to it. The four of us talk, laugh, plan. We

are family. Even during the pandemic, we mask up, maintain social distance, and continue our gathering tradition.

3. Extended family. When Marty married Beth, we got her fab family, and never has there been a better package deal. We got Pearlann and Tom Haines, Beth's smart, fun, parents, and her sister, Stephanie, and brother, Brent, and Brent's wife, Betsy. When they come to visit in a non-pandemic summer, or all come in from Indiana and Chicago for one of Beth's all out pedal-to-the-metal Thanksgivings, it is wonderful.

4. I am Bubby to Beckett and Gavin Graham, and I love them more than I can tell you. They are [almost] four and five years old and the sons of Kent's daughter, Bethany. They keep me laughing, and I love, love, love reading to them. I never had biological children of my own, so this is a gift beyond measure. I am SO grateful to their mom for encouraging and supporting this relationship. She believes, as I do, that a person cannot be loved by too many people.

5. Marty's daughters have been my special loves all their lives. Now they are mothers, and I have a whole new flock of cuties to adore. Charlotte, Blake, Quinn and Sasha share a special place in my heart.

6. Family Zooms! I am one of what was once seventeen first cousins. Three have died, but the other fourteen, their spouses, their children, their children's spouses, and grandchildren are all invited to an extended family Zoom reunion once a month. This is a good thing the pandemic has done.

My capable cousin, Shirley, arranges this, sends out reminders, and hosts the gathering. We cover eight time zones, and just finding a reasonable time for everyone is a challenge. About thirty people attend. I just love seeing everyone, seeing grandchildren I had only heard about. We have to introduce ourselves sometimes to the younger crowd and explain how we are all related. This is why birds flock.

7. Swimming. In another life, I was a pinniped. In the water, my big bulky body can do anything. I stretch out like a lovely, basking on the beach, and swim back and forth, singing along to the songs from my youth playing on my waterproof MP3 player. The sun warms me, the water cools me, my pain vanishes. An hour later, I climb out of the pool a different person than the one who limped to the stairs. I know with every fiber in my body that without this, I would be in a wheelchair. I could not be more grateful to the City of Tallahassee for our wonderful Department of Parks and Recreation.

8. OLLI classes. I rave about OLLI classes all the time, so I am just going to give one illustrative vignette: Professor Allen Romano, classicist extraordinaire, is teaching a class on Zoom on Ovid's Metamorphoses. One of the students in this class is poet David Kirby. We are discussing Daedalus and Icarus. David has found a poem, "Flying not Falling", that points out that Icarus was not a failure: he flew – only eventually flying too close to the sun and melting his wings. David reads a couple of selections from the poem. I have died and gone to heaven. Now *that* is what I call class participation.

9. The color red. I am a lover of vivid color. Cobalt blue and Kelly green have been favorites of mine over the years. I just cannot do dun, tan, sand or beige. I admire it in other people's lives. Not mine. Of late, I am drawn again and again to the kind of ferocious red that we associate with childhood. Red birds, red flowers, red fruit – It sets me on fire and at the same time is playful. It is two faced. Give me red!

10. Older men. A handsome older man is head and shoulders more alluring than some callow fellow. Pretty boys are not to my taste. Older men tend to know exactly what they want and how to get there. No need to elaborate.

11. People who wear masks. I want to feel safe. I want to keep the people around me safe. I want this pandemic to go away. Thank you from the deepest part of my heart for doing this not fun, not glamorous, pain-in-the-ass measure for the good of all of us. Thank you, a thousand times over, for not making a big deal about it.

12. The ever-changing people who shop for and deliver my groceries. You arrive masked and leave the groceries at the end of the driveway for us. I love that you had to check my ID when we bought a six pack of beer. And I love how diligent each of you has been in finding the best produce. You make my life so much safer. Insta-Cart, thank you.

13. Lucilla's Tuesday night supper club. OMG. Every Tuesday night, we get out the good dishes, light candles, and Lucilla's delivers a scrumptious dinner right to the door. If the weather allows, we eat on our screened porch among the orchids. You

bring a bit of glamour and fun into our self-isolating lives. And a LOT of fabulous food. Thank you! Tuesday is now our official favorite day of the week. [Lucilla's stopped the supper club on November 10, but it was wonderful while it lasted.]

14. Girlfriend group phone calls. Once a week. I have told them things I would probably never have told face to face. We laugh, we talk, we are kind to one another. Two Republicans and two Democrats. Yes. The four of us are friends.

15. Resilience. It is amazing what we can survive and endure if we have no other reasonable choice. Yes, I know I am lucky to be relatively safe, although I am ready to opt out of the natural disaster of the month club. I have been through some bad times in my personal life. I lived through 1968. I lived through wars and assassinations, through polio, SARS, Ebola, FLU, AIDS. All of it was scary.

Thank you for my life, for every nook and cranny of it. Thank you, Fate, for my funny far-flung family and friends. There is not one thing that makes me more deserving than others. I am just extraordinarily lucky. And grateful. One day at a time.

Thanksgiving In a Pandemic

We are going to do something death-defying this year: we are joining one other couple for Thanksgiving outdoors, wearing masks, glasses, and gloves. We have spent the last four or five years enjoying a huge blow out Thanksgiving feast with extended family and friends at my brother's house. But because we love those people, we will not be getting together with them next Thursday.

This is not to diminish my love and affection for our hosts this year. They would have been among that happy crowd at Marty's any other year. But this the irony of life in a pandemic. Love someone? Keep your distance. Is Hallmark working on this?

We have all been very, very careful. We have worn masks and tried to distance ourselves. Along with happy anticipation, I have a kernel of dread, a bit of worry about whether we are doing the right thing. Thanksgiving is my second favorite holiday of the year. Passover is the first. I missed that this year, and we will certainly be having the Christmas holidays by Zoom or some other electronic window to the people we miss so much. So, we talked it to death and finally decided to do what we both wanted to do in the first place: join our welcoming friends.

I cannot help but think each year, pandemic or no pandemic, of all the Thanksgivings of the past. Of course, there were wonderful Thanksgivings at my parents' home as I was growing up. Mom had a nuclear family of five to prepare for, and in addition, my military dad brought home those "orphans" on the base who needed a place to chow down and give thanks. Our home, ever open, ever welcoming. Mom just cooked big, and it all disappeared into hungry kids far from home.

When I married my late husband, I got two teenage boys in that bargain. They were all football fans. So, I would post the menu on the fridge door, and we ate in "sittings", carefully timed around halftimes so no one missed a play. It worked beautifully. It also gave us a bit of a pause between courses, and dessert got the separate attention it deserves.

When my brother retired and moved to Tallahassee, my sister-in-law, Beth, turned their home into Turkey Day Central. We have had so much fun and so much food among her extended family and our friends. She's set up long tables, and twenty or more of us would laugh, talk, and indeed be grateful for the candlelight, the pilgrim salt and pepper shakers, the turkey, the something for persons who do not like turkey, the many dishes of sides that looked like carbohydrate heaven, the enormous turkey shaped bowl full of mashed potatoes, the deliciousness of several ovens all set to stun.

And so it is that I anticipate another Thanksgiving with a kind of longing in my heart. Oh, I have so much to be grateful for in this life. I would really need at least a week to celebrate music, books, cats, trees, my wonderful family, my loving husband. But the festival itself, Thanksgiving Day, has become one of the things for which I am so grateful. And of course, I could do this totally alone. Thanks, gratitude, does not require the sacrifice of large fowl. In fact, either you feel it, or you don't. I do, right to the marrow of my bones. I know I live a life of enormous privilege.

So, yes, we will be celebrating Thanksgiving. But no, on second thought as a death-defying act. It will be an affirmation of our happy lives. And safe. Very, very, very safe. That first.

Too Much Information

I have one of those faces: everyone thinks they know me. I have been hugged and kissed by total strangers, and total strangers tell me stuff. Stuff they do not reveal to others. Like the abundance of their spouse's pubic hair.

I was flying out of New York City when a man turned in his seat and shouted down the aisle to his wife that his ears hurt. She was sitting next to me. "It will stop soon," she reassured him.

I looked at the ceiling, checked my seatbelt and rechecked it. Checked the pockets on the back of the seat in front of me. Wife leaned over to me and explained in a voice that would have carried in a sawmill that he had just been "manscaped", and they had waxed his ears. She didn't want everyone to know because it kind of embarrassed him.

"Manscaped?" I said. "Huh. Would you like me to trade seats with your husband?" I asked.

"Heavens no," she said. "Not at all." She then went on to describe manscaping in nitty-gritty detail. Her detailed description caused me to reflect how totally perverse hair growth really is.

We all want hair on our scalps. We do not want hair in our noses, our ears. Mild hair growth for eyebrows and eyelashes can be quite decorative. I do not know a soul who wants hair on his shoulders, back, torso. Pubes should not exceed hair growth. That should be a rule. I tried not to glance over at her husband in a speculative way. I mean, he seemed as typical as a man could who had offered himself up to be manscaped. Tallish, kind of skinny.

You know, of course, that it was the wife who had planned the whole manscaping trip. Located the appropriate "salon", filled out the questionnaire, and explained, again, in detail exactly how she wanted her husband to come out. Her husband had stood nearly naked before a small group of strangers and his wife who discussed in candid terms what they could do with his hopelessly hirsute body. In front of him. It sounded like a P.E. class initiation from middle school.

Apparently, the bulge in his jockey shorts was exuberant pube growth. I wondered for about the tenth time if I knew this woman from somewhere. Surely, a total stranger was not telling me about her husband's pubic hair growth. My eyes shot around the plane looking for a safe place to light. *How did this happen?* I was 20,000 feet in the air, and a total stranger was giving me intimate details about her spouse's body. And then I wondered, *Wait a minute. She may have considered it too much, but what if the problem lay in her desire for someone hairless? What if his manscaping wasn't enough for her? Long soaking baths in some depilatory?* And now, I wanted to size her up.

Nothing about her suggested she allowed a single hair out of place. Her eyebrows were as regimented as red coats. No hair above her lip. She caught me looking. She, too, had just had a thorough waxing and now sported what she called a "landing strip", razored and waxed into her own pubes, she explained. I imagined two tiny men waving bright orange sticks to guide the perfect landing.

I nodded and buried my own imperfectly hairy face in the pages of my book.

Top of the Heap

Send a teacher of the deaf to law school, and the first thing that happens is the fates put a deaf student in her class. Karen was a strikingly beautiful young woman with long blonde hair. She was stunning.

Karen was an oral deaf person, she did not sign, but was an expert lipreader. You might think this is no big deal. It is a very big deal. Something like 80% of all English sounds are made inside the mouth, not on the lips at all. And those sounds that are made on the lips, the bilabials for example, all look alike on the lips. Like P, B, and M. P is made on the lips but is not sounded. Just a puff of air. M is made on the lips and sounded. B is a sounded combination of P and M.

What all this means is that lipreading is an art. Very, very few people who have never heard spoken English can do it at all. Karen was very good at it. But one needs to be close to the instructor, and people speaking all around you, as in a Socratic class, is almost impossible.

I introduced myself after she volunteered in class and her voice told me she was deaf. The professor hesitated just an instant because it was difficult to understand. One to one, it might be fine, but in a huge classroom, it was even more distorted. He got it. And she was right with her answer.

Oh. And it should be obvious: You cannot take notes if you are lipreading.

We decided to try what is called a total communication approach to interpreting. We sat next to one another, and I repeated the lecture, questions, answers on my own lips and through signing. Even though Karen did not sign, they provided more visual clues. We tried it without the signs, but total communication worked best for her.

We had now doubled the number of people who could not take notes. Enter Vivian and Sheila. Sheila's notes were some of the best. We knew because we were all in a study group. Vivian taped each lecture.

Here is how we did it: I interpreted for Karen, Sheila took notes, Vivian taped. At the end of each hour, Vivian gave me her tapes, Sheila gave me her notes, and I took them home, listened to each lecture again, and filled out Sheila's notes. Next day, I xeroxed my annotated notes, making a copy for each of us, and we did it all over again.

We had three or four classes a day, and I can honestly say there was not a single day that I was not exhausted. I could not allow my mind to wander for an instant. The total concentration was tough. And sometimes, Karen would say, "What? What does that mean?" And I would raise my hand and ask.

Karen and I became good friends. I remember we went to a movie together, and we were chatting before the movie started. When the theater darkened, Karen leaned over and said, "Remember, I can't hear you in the dark." And another time, she was laughing, and her hearing aids were making beeping noises because the movement of her face had caused the aids to move inside her ear canals. She said, "I beep when I smile." She was an absolute delight. Smart as a whip and strong in a way few could ever be. Nothing was easy for her, nothing. But she was always top of the heap.

Our first year, we had assigned classes. Karen and I, Vivian and Sheila could work our exhausting magic. But second year, we had some choice in classes. I quickly realized that Karen was choosing classes I chose which was horribly unfair to her.

We went to see the dean to ask about the school's responsibility in finding an interpreter. We had a new dean who, at first, escorted us out of his office saying something to the effect that we could sue the school if we wanted. As we had been nothing but cordial and polite, we were nonplussed. A passing faculty member saw us in the hall and asked what was wrong and got it all sorted for us. Karen got a paid interpreter. And she got to study the parts of the law that were important to her.

The school awarded me the Tubbs Award for my efforts. But I could not have done this without the help of Sheila and Vivian. They should have shared in the award. Karen went on to get an advanced degree in law in the area of taxation. She practices in Central Florida.

Tri-Hi-Y

In my new high school, a friendly girl in my homeroom suggested I come to Tri-Hi-Y with her. "It's a girls' club," she said. "Lots of fun." So, I went. They were planning a hayride, and I was totally in with that.

Our meetings began with a reading from Kahlil Gibran's *The Prophet* or perhaps some poetry. Then we gabbed, planned another social event like Sadie Hawkins Day, and generally just enjoyed the companionship. Eventually, I was elected Chaplain of this group and continued with the Gibran poetry readings of my predecessors in that post. I enjoyed the club and stayed in until I graduated. For the entirety of my junior and senior years, I was "Chaplain". Not once did anyone tell me that this was a Christian girls' organization. As a Jewish girl, this might have been good information to have. But if they didn't care, neither did I.

In the spring of the year, we were all sitting in homeroom, listening to the principal's morning announcements over the PA system. He surprised me by announcing that I had won a $500 scholarship to be awarded by the D.A.R., Daughters of the American Revolution. [Or maybe it was the Daughters of the Confederacy. I truly do not remember.] I was? Really? I couldn't wait to get home and tell my parents.

I was surprised at my parents' reaction. They smiled tentatively and said, "Are you sure?" They gave one another one of those looks that means they are not telling all they know. I called my friend from across the street to come over and confirm the morning's announcement. He did. My parents said, "Well, we'll see."

The next morning, one of the guidance counselors pulled me out of class to speak privately with me in the hall. She was whispering. "Paula", she asked, "are you Jewish? I'm so sorry I have to ask this."

"Yes." I didn't hesitate. "I'm Jewish."

"But you are the Chaplain of Tri-Hi-Y!" She was clearly upset about this news which completely flabbergasted me. In retrospect, maybe she thought that I was masquerading as something I am not, "passing" as a Christian.

I never heard another word about the scholarship. If my parents heard from someone at the school, they never mentioned it. But at the senior awards ceremony, a new award was initiated: a citizenship award to someone selected by the teachers. I was chosen. My consolation prize.

I may sound ungrateful to whomever arranged for this "award". I knew it was insincere. Something concocted out of thin air to console both me and them. What it really did was confirm in my mind something my mother had been trying to tell me for years: "You must know yourself. If you do not know who you are, other people will tell you who you are and what you are. Know yourself." It was a public learning experience.

Covid Chronicles 10: 7/12/20

I have a confession to make. I am adjusting to this new life. When I retired in 2012, I downsized to a little hobbit hole that has all my favorite things in it. Everywhere my eye lights, there is another memory.

Although I gave away hundreds of books in '12, I have accumulated many more. My music is here and accessible in every room. Even my porch. I have a television set and an absurd number of channels and sites to watch series, movies, documentaries, HAMILTON! It is nothing fancy, but our hobbit hole fits us to a tee. Spending time in it is wonderful. I planned it that way years before the plague came knocking at our door.

I leave this nest for one hour each day to go to the public pool on John Knox Road. The pools are still closed for general swimming, but you can call and make a reservation to lap swim or water walk for an hour. I do that. The water transports me to Paula Place where I just concentrate on my exercise and sing along with my MP3 player. Sixty minutes every day. Rain or shine. That is the only time I am not at home.

I spend quite a bit of time on Zooms and conference calls with groups of friends. It is different than being together. But different is okay. I hear their distinctive voices, see them with their plague hairdos, and they see mine. Groceries are ordered online and delivered to the door. The good people at Amazon send their smiling boxes to us almost every day. Things we would have picked up at the drugstore or any other store are delivered to us. I have to stop and remember what day of the week it is. My son says there is daytime then nighttime, rinse and repeat.

There are two lovely creatures who are my nearly constant companions in all this. The first is the world's most adorable tuxedo cat, Figaro. He brings us live creatures from the wider world of our neighborhood and sleeps beside me companionably while I read.

But the real stalwart, the linchpin, the keystone to plague world is Kent Ross Putnam, my husband. He wakes up happy to be alive and talks me off the ledge when the horrors outside start to close in. Before this sheltering in place, he enjoyed traveling, and I encouraged him to do it. I traveled a lot in my life, and although I can't do it now, I wanted that joy for him. And he loves it. But that joy is closed to him right now, so I am just loving having his bright company. There is nothing like being happily married to get you through a crisis. More Kent? Yes, please. And he doesn't complain about his changed world. He adapts. He is resilient. I wish for him a return to the life he loved.

And I have this old computer. I sit here and muse about life, about how it turned on a dime. And I write these notes for myself and hoping that someone will read this computer-generated note in a bottle and send me back a note about their lives. How are you adapting? Or I take a walk down memory lane.

I have so many memories! Why I walked into the kitchen is not one of them. This life is doable. What will be next?

About the Author

Paula Walborsky is a recovering family law attorney who lives in Tallahassee, Florida with her husband, Kent Putnam. The two of them serve as indulgent staff to their cat, Figaro.

* * *

If you enjoyed *Unpacking Paula: Volume I*, **please leave a review on Amazon** and/or Goodreads. I'll be eternally grateful. 😊

Warmly,

Paula

Made in United States
Orlando, FL
06 May 2024